WALKING IN RUINS

also by GEOFF NICHOLSON

The Lost Art of Walking
Gravity's Volkswagen
Sex Collectors
The Hollywood Dodo
Bedlam Burning
Female Ruins
Flesh Guitar
Bleeding London
Footsucker
Everything and More
Still Life with Volkswagens
The Errol Flynn Novel
Day Trips to the Desert
The Food Chain
Hunters and Gatherers
Big Noises
What We Did on Our Holidays
The Knot Garden
Street Sleeper

Walking in Ruins

GEOFF NICHOLSON

HARBOUR

First published as a paperback original by Harbour in 2013
Harbour Books (East) Ltd, PO Box 10594
Chelmsford, Essex CM1 9PB
info@harbourbooks.co.uk

A CIP record for this book is available
from the British Library

ISBN 978 190512820 4

Typeset in Great Britain by Antony Gray
Printed and bound in Finland by Bookwell

Contents

1

Just What is it that Makes Today's Ruins so Different, so Appealing? An Introduction.

Ruin hath taught me thus to ruminate,
That Time will come and take my love away.
  This thought is as a death, which cannot choose
  But weep to have that which it fears to lose.

William Shakespeare, Sonnet 64

What are we doing?
We're sitting on a ruin.

Cat Power, 'Ruin'

I was walking in Jaywick, on the south coast of Essex, a town that people had been telling me about for years, describing it as weird, gloomy, bleak, melancholy, isolated, vaguely threatening: all the things I love and am drawn to. Jaywick was built in the 1930s as a holiday resort for London's Eastenders, but according to a government survey with the title 'Indices of Multiple Deprivation', it has for some time been the most deprived spot in England. This particular survey factors in statistics for income, employment, health, disability, crime and living standards; and no doubt the place was full of poor, sick, unemployed people, some of them victims of crime, some of them presumably criminals. Even so, if the large number of caravans dotting the landscape was anything to go by, a lot of people still wanted to be there, at least for part of the year. You also had to wonder how a government survey might factor in weirdness, gloom, bleakness, melancholy, isolation, vague threat. I'll bet they didn't even try.

Jaywick is not by any means a wholly ruined town, but it is a town that contains plenty of ruined buildings, some of them formerly quaint, charming, miniature seaside cottages or chalets. A man with a taste for ruin might find himself strangely moved by these dwellings that had been abandoned, smashed up, sprayed with ambitionless graffiti, in some cases completely burned out. He might be equally moved by other houses, nestling all too close to the ruins, that were clearly the homes of the neat, the well organised, the house-proud. Next to the burned-out shells there were often beautifully painted clapboard homes, with gardens full of neat flowerbeds, sometimes decorated with leprechauns and wishing wells. There was certainly some received wisdom going around that the house wreckers and ruiners would eventually prevail, though equally there was a campaign to revitalise the town, run by the Jaywick Tourist Board: their slogan, 'Jaywick, wicked!'

I was walking there to satisfy my curiosity, I had no grand walking project in mind. Most of the streets of Jaywick were empty and unpopulated, but along the main thoroughfare, Broadway, between the houses and the high sea wall, I encountered more than one shaven-headed man, a can of extra-strong lager occupying one hand, a dog on a string occupying the other. One of them stopped to rifle through every rubbish bin he passed, which required much juggling and repositioning of can and dog, and frankly it didn't seem he was finding any treasures in those bins. I wouldn't say these guys were warm and welcoming, but the nods they gave me were of grudging recognition rather than open hostility. Maybe they had me down as some effete popinjay from the metropolis, but at least I'd got enough nous and nerve to walk the mean streets of their town.

I threaded my way through the side streets again, looking at

some of the charming and some of the charmless little dwellings, and I came across a small bungalow with a pitched roof and a square extension built out the back, pressed up against a low wooden fence. There was a window in the back of the extension, six panes of glass, a couple of them boarded up, one replaced with blue glass, one with a lace curtain across it. And on the wall below the window somebody had painted, with a brush rather than a spray can, in big, misshapen, irregular letters, the message B.AWARE of thE DOG'Z.

Was this really as lame as it looked, just somebody's attempt to warn off trespassers? Maybe, but wasn't painting something so ugly on your own house a bit idiotic? Or was it cleverer than it looked, in fact saying, 'Look, I'm crazy enough to vandalise the exterior of my own home, you'd better not mess with me'? Or had it not been done by the house owner, was it a graffito? Were the DOG'Z a gang, a band, a set of rappers, a posse? Was the whole thing some very smart Banksy-esque pastiche of tagger stupidity? I don't expect ever to know.

* * *

A little while later I was in Barstow, in California. If Barstow is known at all, it's from the opening of Hunter S. Thompson's *Fear and Loathing in Las Vegas*: 'We were somewhere around Barstow, on the edge of the desert, when the drugs began to take hold.' It's a great line, but one that raises a few questions, I think. By the time you get to Barstow you're already well beyond the desert edge, you're in the desert proper, and if you've driven there from Los Angeles, and took the drugs as you set off, and Hunter S. never struck me as a man with a taste for delayed gratification, they'd certainly have taken hold a good while earlier.

I go to Barstow once in a while, not for the drugs, but because it's a good place to start from if you want to do some desert walking, which I sometimes do. Barstow itself isn't most people's idea of a walking town. Temperatures rise to the low hundreds in July and August, and the main drag is long, pretty steep in places, with wide gaps between the various, not especially enticing, motels, fast-food joints, gas stations and under-stocked supermarkets, and in certain stretches there are as many closed-down stores as there are open ones. The Barstow walker is often short of diversions.

Even so, you do see a surprising number of people walking along, and most of them don't look like they've had much choice in the matter. They're walking because they're poor, without cars and sometimes without homes. They look like they've been that way for a good long time, and that nothing's going to change in the near future. They look, essentially, ruined. Some, no doubt, were recent, and possibly future, inmates of the local Barstow Jail. Also, in a Woody Guthrie-ish throwback, Barstow is still a hub for people who like to hop freight cars and ride the rails. Really.

Some of the older Barstow residents I've talked to tell me how much better the town used to be, that it's been ruined by drugs, crime and illegal immigration. Standards and house prices have plummeted, but as is the way with these things, it's always hard for people to say exactly when this golden age actually was. I've been going there for thirty years or so now, and I don't recall it ever being anything but a rough old place: that was the attraction.

Barstow came into existence as a railroad centre. It's no longer as big or as busy as it used to be – the grand station remains but there are no passenger trains passing through, and some of the tracks are gone – but Barstow is still very much in the railroad business. There are still substantial marshalling yards, and immensely long freight trains snake through the outskirts of the town all the time. Barstow's railyard emits more diesel pollution than any other yard in the state, which creates significant health risks for people living alongside the tracks in Barstow, though I think the people living alongside the tracks have plenty of other things to worry about. Nevertheless, life of a certain sort definitely thrives and clings around Barstow's railroad tracks.

I like to walk around Barstow early in the morning, when the sun is low and cool, when the shadows are long, the distant, pale blue and grey desert hills look quite beautiful, and the few people on the street have no particular interest in the solitary walker. Last time I was there I took a walk along East Main, over the rail bridge, with a dozen or more tracks curling gently below, and on the other side I came to a line of broken-down shacks and houses, across from the old station. This was my kind of territory, the kind of place I like to walk and poke around; many of the buildings certainly looked like ruins, although some didn't, not quite, or at least not yet. As I walked towards them, I realised it was impossible to tell which houses were likely to be inhabited, which ones were genuine ruins. One of the most derelict-looking, I discovered, was home to a large and essentially cheerful Latino family who were every bit as surprised by my sudden presence as I was by theirs.

I walked back to the main strip, through a parking lot adjacent to the Desert Motel, by no means the worst looking motel in town. As I went alongside it, I saw a number of No Trespassing signs, different shapes and sizes, one of them perforated with bullet holes. And just to hammer home the message, painted on the wooden boundary fence by someone who might easily have some kin over in Jaywick, was the warning BE-WARE OF THE WILD DOG. Who knew that 'beware' would present such problems to the uncertain speller? This one definitely wasn't a Banksy-esque pastiche, or the name of a band or posse; the motel management really didn't want anybody poking around behind their motel. You could understand that. On the other hand I didn't really imagine there actually was a wild dog loose in the motel grounds; at the very least wouldn't that be bad for business? I certainly saw no sign of a dog, any more than I saw one behind the bungalow in Jaywick. Neither Barstow nor Jaywick is strictly speaking a ghost town, but maybe both have ghost dogs.

* * *

If, like me, you're the author of a book titled *The Lost Art of Walking*, and therefore have some reputation as a walker, people tend to ask you, 'What's your favourite walk?' I always find this an excruciatingly difficult question. I want to answer honestly, want to give a reasonable reply, and I definitely don't want to be evasive or pretentious or precious, but the answer constantly eludes me.

Naturally there are certain walks I do all the time, specific routes in my own neighbourhood, which, for reasons that seem more explicable on some days than others, is currently East Hollywood, in Los Angeles, California; admittedly not most people's idea of a great place to walk, though I'm prepared to argue about that. I vary these walks as much as I can, but at this point I've lived here long enough to reckon, without being smug about it, that I'm pretty well familiar with all the streets and routes that could possibly constitute a local walk, the ones I can do simply by setting off from my own front door. Sometimes these individual walks are combined, or extended, when I feel especially like walking, or when there are guests in town and I want to give them a thorough walking tour of the area, and inevitably there are still occasional surprises, things I hadn't noticed before or things that have changed. Are these favourite walks? Well, they're certainly the walks I do most often, often enough fot there to be a pleasant familiarity about them, and familiarity isn't to be despised, but I never exactly chose them. I do them largely because they're *there*, which is perhaps to say that I do them because I'm *here*.

When I go back to London, the city where I have lived and walked longer than any other, more than twenty years, I sometimes have a specific walking project in mind, but there are certain places I always walk, through habit mostly, even when not consciously 'going for a walk': Charing Cross Road, Soho, Smithfield Market, Lambeth Bridge, the Harrow Road – places I worked or lived, where I had and in some cases still have friends, or places where I simply walked for no good reason at all.

In New York, the city where I lived after leaving London and before moving to Los Angeles, there's a stretch of Broadway between 48th Street and Canal that I always end up walking because it was a walk I used to do all the time when I lived there. I'd get off the bus at Port Authority, walk up to the guitar stores and press my nose against the glass, then head downtown to SoHo, where my wife's office used to be. I also find myself walking on the Bowery, and across Brooklyn Bridge, and these days when visiting Manhattan it seems obligatory to walk down to Ground Zero.

None of these walks is random or accidental. I could choose not to walk in these places, and the fact that I don't make that choice suggests I actually do like walking there. And in many cases I'm performing an act of memory as much as of pedestrianism. I look at the way things are, and think about the way things used to be, what's still there, what's disappeared, what's been spoiled, how much has changed – including my own personality, habits and tastes. It's all very Wordsworthian: very 'Tintern Abbey'. Certainly these walks are enjoyable in the broadest sense, but I'm not sure it has much to do with 'favouritism'.

* * *

There's another problem too. The person who asks me about my favourite walk is often looking for a recommendation, for a route they might walk themselves. I'm reluctant to make that kind of recommendation, because in most cases I don't know the person very well, in some cases not at all. I don't know their tastes, their preferences, their stamina. It's like having some stranger ask you to recommend a book. Well, *Moby Dick*'s a good read; but you don't need me to tell you that. There's a cracking walk to be done along the Pennine Way or the Great Wall of China; but again, everybody knows that already.

Sometimes I fudge the whole thing and go the Zen, mystical route. I say that my favourite walk is the one I'm about to do next, or, depending on the circumstances, the walk I'm doing at that very moment. It's true as far as it goes. I, along with most walkers I know, walk for the joy of walking as much as because they want to look at the scenery, and even less because they want to get somewhere. The meander is the message. Even so, we know that not all walks are created equal. Some walks are simply 'better' than others, they provide more possibilities, more satisfaction, more *entertainment*. And this is where an even bigger problem occurs

Increasingly I find that if I'm in an area of unspoiled natural beauty, or in a major city full of great vistas and magnificent architecture, I may be impressed, I may well be appreciative, I'm certainly not dismissive, and this is never 'bad' walking territory, but the truth is I'm often slightly bored in these places. Only a fool would bad-mouth the Champs-Élysées or the Lake District, but I just don't get very excited at the prospect of walking there. Whereas if I'm walking along a beach and discover a ruined pier or some wrecked beach houses, or if I'm at the edge of a city and find a disused warehouse or factory, then I'm fascinated, I'm thrilled, I'm moved. I feel like I'm in my element. The fact is: what I love best is walking in ruins.

One thing that makes this easier, once you've got the idea in your head, is that you really don't have to go looking for ruin, you can find it just about anywhere. Sure, the Acropolis is a fine place to walk, and I remember a great afternoon plodding around the Roman ruins in Volubilis in Morocco, but there's absolutely no need to go that far. Set out walking just about anywhere and the chances are that before very long you'll come across some form of ruin, be it a derelict house or a wrecked barn, a crumbling greenhouse or the shell of some petrol station, a patch of blighted beach, an abandoned quarry.

There's a house right here in my own neighbourhood, known to some locals as the Haunted House. It was evidently once a substantial dwelling, more rustic than is usual in these parts – it would look perfectly at home in the middle of a pine forest – but it still shows its elegance, built on the top of a steep slope, with wooden clapboard walls, overhanging timber decks and balconies. It's been empty for a good long time, and nobody I've talked to knows the complete story of who the owners are, when and why they moved away, or why they won't sell, restore or even demolish it. Somebody has suggested a murder was committed inside, but that's just urban legend as far as I can tell. It's now in an advanced though not necessarily terminal state of decay, though I'm not sure there are many who would want to take it on as a project. Adolescents get up to low-level criminality in and around it, though you don't get the sense that it's completely abandoned:

somebody evidently comes round once in a while, repairs the fence, clears up the beer bottles, paints over the graffiti.

Every time I walk past it, I get a little kick of excitement. I see there's a little more decay, more crumbling, less paint on the walls, the decks look less solid, one of the balconies has a hole in it and is gradually detaching itself from the back wall: it's literally falling apart. I love having it there and being able to walk by it, though I suppose I wouldn't want to live next door to it, more because of the beer-drinking, dope-smoking, graffiti-drawing kids than because of any imagined hauntings. It definitely won't be there for ever, but who would have it any other way? Sooner or later it will slide all the way down the hill, and at that point it will become much more ruined, but perhaps less of a ruin. It will become just a heap of building materials. That'll be fine too. The best ruins always demonstrate transience, although some also demonstrate resilience, staying power.

One short walk I like to take in the City of London, for instance, takes me past two ruined churches, St Dunstan-in-the-East and Christ Church Greyfriars, both bombed out in the Blitz and both now preserved in their partial state as war memorials. Walking from one to the other usually involves going by St Paul's Cathedral, by no means a ruin, but nevertheless pitted with World War II shrapnel scars. A short detour takes you to the twice-relocated ruins of the Roman temple of Mithras. It isn't too much of a challenge to find some London ruins to walk in.

On the west side of Manhattan there is the High Line, a defunct section of the elevated railway, once a ruin where an intrepid soul did occasionally walk but now converted into a long, thin pedestrian zone so that walkers can stroll high above ground level and look down on the poor suckers beneath them. New Yorkers seem justifiably proud of the High Line and a lot of people, no doubt some of them out-of-towners, do walk there with great enthusiasm, but it's a very specific kind of walking, actually I think more a form of promenading. People walking up and down, savouring the pleasure of walking, looking around, showing themselves off, checking each other out: very old school. Few, if any, of these people are using the High Line as a way of getting from A to B. The place functions as a kind of pedestrian theme park, a piece of reclaimed territory, decked out with designer sidewalks and exuberant landscaping while keeping some of the old rails still visible.

The first couple of times I went to the High Line, a small industrial building was being demolished very close to the southern end of the walkway. Just one man was doing the job, operating a surprisingly small machine, one with a single long arm with an hydraulic hammer on the end, something that looked like a giant hole punch. Smashing walls and roofs was easy enough but once in a while the operator encountered metal girders that were much harder to break down, resulting in an explosion of grinding and juddering, though he always got the job done sooner or later. The whole process delivered quite an ear-bashing to the walkers on the High Line, and clouds of demolition dust rose up and billowed in our direction. The noise and the dirt were the kind of thing that you might think would spoil a good walk. But it didn't. I, naturally, absolutely loved it, but so did most of the other walkers. We paused in our walking, moved to the side of the High Line, pressed up against the railing and stared down in fascination to see how one man could destroy a whole building. A certain amount of ruin, the chance to see a ruin being made, didn't spoil the walk at all: it made it. If I'm ever called upon to design a pedestrian theme park I'll make sure there's some industrial-scale destruction going on there.

* * *

So, to come back to the initial question, when people ask me to name a favourite walk and offer a recommendation, I increasingly want to say: 'You should really go to Jaywick and walk around the burned-out houses and look at the demented graffiti;' or, 'You should walk in some place where you can see buildings being demolished.' But I don't. I'm a reasonable man, and I don't want people to think I'm nuts. I'm more likely to say that the Peak District is pretty great, or that a stroll through Brooklyn's Prospect Park is very enjoyable. I'm not exactly lying, but I am faking, giving people the answer I think they want.

And I do wonder *why* I'm so drawn to ruin, to decay, to desolation, why I want to walk around old mills, junkyards, ghost towns, broken-down caravan sites; even 'preserved' ruins, castles, stone circles, battlefields, decommissioned military sites. And I thought I might begin by asking how far back it goes. Quite a way, it seems.

* * *

I have a snapshot taken of me when I was a kid, definitely not more than ten years old, standing beside a ruined stone tower, looking like the king of the castle. I have no memory of it being taken, nor much idea of where that tower is. I would guess it's somewhere in Derbyshire, possibly in Lathkill Dale: that was a place my family went once in a while and there are some ruined buildings there, the remains of a lead-ore operation, but they don't look much like the ones in the photograph, to be honest. Still, wherever it was taken, I wonder if it's possible that I responded to something in that ruin and asked my father to take the picture. Maybe, though it's just as likely that it was his own idea and I simply stood where I was told to. Either way I'm not inclined to read too much into it. The first serious encounter with ruins that I fully remember came later, but it also involved photography and my father.

When I was in my mid-teens, in Sheffield, in the late 1960s, I was a sufficiently keen amateur photographer to persuade my parents to buy me a 'serious' camera. My mother had a part-time job at a camera shop, and could get a discount, and so I became the owner of a Zenith B, a Russian camera, crude, clunky, heavy as a brick, but a genuine single-lens reflex, and perfectly good enough for my ultimately not-all-that-serious needs.

New camera slung weightily over my shoulder, I took a bus to the other side of the city, to Broomhill, a district John Betjeman wrote a poem about (containing the remarkable couplet 'But in our arboreta / The sounds are discreeter') and which he described as 'the prettiest suburb in England'. I spent an afternoon walking around, photographing this and that, and in due course I had the film processed, and after I'd got the prints back I showed the results to my father, though by then I'd learned not to expect much enthusiasm from him about any of the things I did. The pictures I showed him were taken in and around some ruined buildings: houses, workshops, a small factory.

'So,' my father said gruffly, 'there's a lot of derelict property in Broomhill is there?'

I'm still not sure whether this was a dismissive put-down or a genuine enquiry. At the time, being a sullen adolescent, I naturally took it to be the former. Now it doesn't seem such a bad question. And the answer would have been no, that there really wasn't so very much derelict property in Broomhill. It was, and remains, the pleasant, prosperous, leafy suburb that Betjeman knew, but I'd found the half-dozen or so examples of ruin and trained my photographic gaze on them. Why? Because I thought that was the kind of thing a photographer was supposed to take pictures of. Ruins were picturesque, a suitable subject for serious photography, for serious art in general.

Today I wonder exactly where I got that idea. True I had seen the movie *The Last Days of Pompeii*, a sword-and-sandal extravaganza starring Steve Reeves, part-written by Sergio Leone.

I had certainly been to the local art gallery and museum, and I'm sure there must have been some paintings there that depicted ruins, though I can't recall any specific examples. I was also discovering the adolescent joys of Surrealism, in books rather than on any gallery wall, and I had seen ruins in paintings by De Chirico, Dali and Delvaux.

I'm pretty sure I'd never been to a proper photographic exhibition at that time, but I had seen the magazine *Amateur Photographer*: my mother used to bring home free copies from her camera shop. I'd also been in the public library and leafed through the annuals published by the *British Journal of Photography*, collections of the year's 'best pictures'. I don't think I'd seen the actual work of Walker Evans or Ansel Adams, Edward Weston or Dorothea Lange, but I'd seen lots of work by their admirers and imitators.

In these magazines and annuals, alongside already very dated-looking images of babies and children, close-ups of rocks or tree trunks, portraits of craggy-faced 'characters', an occasional tasteful nude, all of them in black and white, there'd always be a photograph or two of a ruin, generally something elegant and classical, from Rome or Greece, Mayan at a pinch. I'm pretty sure I'd also seen one or two photographs that combined both nudity and ruin, though I'm sure that at that point in my life the nudity would have been infinitely more compelling than the ruin.

No doubt all this played a part in my appreciation of, and respect for, ruin but the fact was that in Sheffield there was no need for the aestheticisation of ruin; it was an everyday reality. We were still near enough to the Second World War for the imagery of bombings and their aftermath to be part of the public consciousness and of the shared iconography, though I doubt that many Sheffielders would have put it that way. The playground at my junior school was edged with a line of boarded-up, but intact, air-raid shelters. You could be perfectly familiar with, say, the London Blitz photographs of Bill Brandt and Cecil Beaton without being at all interested in photography *per se*, much less interested in ruins, and you certainly didn't have to know who Bill Brandt and Cecil Beaton were.

Sheffield had had a blitz of its own, short-lived and limited by some standards, by London's certainly, just two raids in December 1940, but that was enough to terrorise the citizens of Sheffield, who'd known for some time what was coming. And when it came, nearly seven hundred people were killed, another fifteen hundred injured, and large swathes of the city were destroyed, leaving tens of thousands homeless. The steel-works and munitions factories that had been the prime targets for the raids suffered comparatively little damage. These events remained fresh in the minds of my parents' and their parents' generations, and were a continuing source of tragic, heroic and sometimes comic anecdotes; and they passed these stories, along with a fair amount of dread, on to me.

There was a story current in our family that my father, then aged fifteen (pretty much the same age I was when I went photographing ruin in Broomhill), had walked to work the morning after the first round of Sheffield bombings, stepping over debris and, according to my mother, also over dead bodies. My father never mentioned it at all, which I've always thought gives the story more rather than less credibility, but I may be wrong.

As I was growing up in Sheffield, any patches of waste ground around the city were casually referred to as 'bomb-sites', but although I'm sure some literally were – it took a long time to clean up and revitalise the city – I'm equally sure that some were not. The term was loosely applied to any kind of neglect or mess. When my own bedroom was particularly chaotic, my mother would say it looked like a bomb-site, or as if a bomb had hit it. Eventually, continuing my role as sullen adolescent, I pointed out that if a real bomb had actually hit my bedroom then I really wouldn't have to make my bed or pick up my dirty socks, would I now?

There's also some suggestion that Sheffield waste ground was uniquely ruined, even before the German bombs got to it. In 1937 in *The Road to Wigan Pier*, George Orwell wrote:

> One particular picture of Sheffield stays by me. A frightful piece of waste ground (somehow, up here a piece of waste ground attains a squalor that would be impossible even in London), trampled quite bare of grass and littered with newspaper, old saucepans, etc. To the right an isolated row of gaunt four-room houses, dark red, blackened by smoke. To the left an interminable vista of factory chimneys, chimney behind chimney, fading away into a dim blackish haze. Behind me a railway embankment made from the slag of furnaces . . .

The implication is that Sheffield looked like a ruin long before it was ruined by German air raids, and even as successful post-war attempts were made to rebuild and revitalise it, slums, dereliction, bomb damage, remained a part of the scenery.

In 1941, the year after he'd walked through the ruins of Sheffield, my father volunteered for the navy and went to fight in the war. I have no idea precisely which or how many ruins he saw during his service: he never talked about that either, but afterwards he became a joiner, a builder, working for Sheffield Corporation, involved with the rebuilding of the city. And if it's a bit of a stretch to think that he choose that career as a direct result of having seen the destruction caused by war, I think he was certainly pleased to be involved in creating rather than destroying.

In Sheffield, not only did the buildings bombed in the blitz have to be replaced, the city also embarked on a massive slum-

Photograph © Sheffield Newspapers/ Sheffield Pictures

clearance programme and another much needed programme to clean up the legendary air pollution. You didn't need an eye as sharp as Orwell's to see that something had to be done about the ruined state of Sheffield. So perhaps these are all good reasons why I was attracted to the ruins of Broomhill, and why my father looked at the photographs I took that day and saw them as derelict buildings that required work, that needed to be restored or replaced. He couldn't see them as examples of the picturesque, as beautiful ruins.

* * *

There are a lot of extant pictures of the Sheffield blitz, though I can't find any of them credited to a named photographer. There was no Sheffield equivalent of Bill Brandt or Cecil Beaton as far as I can tell. The vast majority of the photographs, like the one above, found in the Sheffield Library archives, are simply credited to 'Sheffield Newspapers'.

This is the best known, and I think the best, photograph from the Sheffield blitz. It shows the High Street on fire, a couple of abandoned trams silhouetted against the conflagration. Other photographs exist of the scene, taken that night and the next morning, and from other angles, but none look as dramatic, as 'good' as this.

I've looked at a lot of photographs of ruins in the course of writing this book. It's generally reckoned that the earliest photograph of any historical event was taken in May 1842 by C. F. Stelzner: it's a daguerreotype showing the ruins of Hamburg after a devastating fire. That photograph didn't make it into the papers however. The *Illustrated London News* ran some pictures of the event but they used an old print of Hamburg, obtained from the British Museum, and then had an artist paint smoke and flames over it. There are no figures visible in the Stelzner photograph – they would have had to stand still for a very long time before the camera could register them – but the fact is that while an image of ruins is all well and good, an image of somebody walking in those ruins really takes things up a level; it adds scale, human interest, as well as a compositional element.

So I look at that picture from the Sheffield blitz and I wonder about that solitary, silhouetted figure by the lamp-post about a quarter of the way in from the right. Who is he? A passer-by? An air-raid warden? What's he doing there? He looks so untroubled, so at ease, perhaps strutting slightly; and the strut would certainly be in keeping with what we're told about air-raid wardens. But where could he possibly be walking to so casually in the middle, or even in the aftermath, of an air raid? And I wonder if he was placed there by the photographer, for the sake of the shot. So maybe he isn't walking but posing, only pretending to walk, standing where the photographer told him to stand. I even wonder if perhaps he was the photographer's assistant.

There is some precedent for this. The well-known photograph opposite by Fred Morley, taken on 9 October 1940, shows a cheery young milkman walking through the rubble of London the morning after a bombing raid. The photograph was shot for

Photograph © Hulton-Deutsch Collection/CORBIS

the agency Fox Photos. The street in fact looks more or less impassable, and a couple of firemen are visible hosing down a building in the background. I'd been aware of the photograph for some time, and I always thought it was probably a set-up, though not a particularly reprehensible one, simply a morale-boosting image to show that London life was still going on normally even after a night of bombings. For one thing, I found it hard to believe that milkmen were sticking to their rounds in the days of the Blitz. Would there even be any doorsteps to leave the milk on? And when the milkman came back at the end of the week to collect his money, what were the chances of the customers still being there, what possible likelihood that they'd hand over what they owed?

But it turns out the photograph is much more fake than I thought. It's widely reported that the 'milkman' was Fred Morley's assistant, dressed up for the part. Fair enough, but that raises more questions than it answers. Because obviously the assistant or the photographer must have borrowed the coat and the crate of milk from somebody, and if not from an actual milkman, then from whom? So does that mean there really *were* milkmen making deliveries? And if so, why didn't Morley use a real milkman in the photograph? Couldn't he find one winsome or perky enough? Or did the real milkmen think this photography lark was an insult, and refuse to appear in a set-up photograph? But if so, surely they wouldn't have lent the jacket and bottles of milk, would they? Or were there perhaps no real milkmen involved at all, and did the photographer bring the jacket and milk with him as props? It's generally assumed that the firemen working in the background are the genuine article, and that being so I can imagine they might be extremely pissed off that this photographer and his assistant were free to lark about smiling, posing, taking pictures, while they had real work to do. Didn't the photographer know there was a war on?

* * *

I can only imagine how it would feel to drop bombs on an 'enemy', to create ruin. However, there's plenty of evidence to suggest that a lot of people can do it without feeling especially bad afterwards. I suppose you tell yourself that you're only doing to them what they'd happily do to you. You're trying to win a war. You have a mission. You want to do a good job. And leaving a set of ruins is a pretty clear indication of a job well done.

Paul Tibbets, who flew the Enola Gay (named after his mother) and dropped the first atomic bomb on Hiroshima, said (how truthfully we can only surmise) that he never lost a single night's sleep after the mission. In a 1975 interview he said, 'I'm not proud that I killed eighty thousand people, but I'm proud that I was able to start with nothing, plan it and have it work as perfectly as it did.' He also said, 'If Dante had been with us on the plane, he would have been terrified. The city we had seen so clearly in the sunlight a few minutes before was now an ugly smudge. It had completely disappeared under this awful blanket of smoke and fire.' In a 2002 interview Studs Terkel asked him, 'Do you have any idea what happened down below?' Tibbets replied, 'Pandemonium'. I'd suggest that a bomber pilot who references both Dante and Milton in interviews is a man who may have given at least some thought to the nature of ruin. 'Now I am become Death, the destroyer of worlds.' Well, only up to a point.

The building that was the target of the Hiroshima raid, the Industrial Promotion Hall, was not completely destroyed in the bombing. Even though and indeed because, the atomic bomb exploded immediately above it, parts of the building survived, though all the people inside were instantly killed. The ruined building has now become the Hiroshima Peace Memorial, also known as the Atomic Bomb Dome. It's now set in a large park, surrounded by walking paths. Photographs suggest that the dome is rather more impressive as a ruin than it was as a functioning building. As a complete structure it was chunky, ponderous, with the dome looking like an afterthought. But as a ruin it's a wonder, a castle, a fortress. The heavy walls are opened up, light gleams through the window openings; the glass of the dome is gone, of course, but the curved struts remain and have a lightness and a geometrical grace to them.

Paul Tibbets, naturally, did not walk in Hiroshima, but British troops were on the ground there just a few weeks after the bombing, to rebuild part of the city's infrastructure. One of them at least, Sapper Ronald Taylor, walked the streets and photographed the ruins. The photographs were only found after his death by his grandson, who duly made them public. The *Daily Mail* published some of the images in an article headlined, 'Walking Through a Nuclear Winter'.

Taylor's photographs are haunting and moving: the city is reduced to a bare, grey, horizontal plane. But none of the shots I've seen show the building that has become the Hiroshima

Peace Memorial, that would at the time simply have been called the ruins of the Industrial Promotion Hall. Perhaps in those weeks that Sapper Taylor walked the streets of Hiroshima it was too early to see the building's symbolic potential. Or perhaps Sapper Taylor simply didn't walk in that part of town. By 1953, when Alain Resnais made the movie *Hiroshima Mon Amour*, from a script by Marguerite Duras, it was certainly a ruin freighted with broad and heavy symbolism (though, lord knows, many things are in Alain Resnais's movies), and much in evidence as the hero and heroine walk the city, but it wasn't until 1966 that the Hiroshima Council passed a resolution that the dome should be preserved in perpetuity.

Well, perpetuity is a very long time and of course a problem in that it creates a paradox that affects all 'preserved' ruins. At what point do we put a ruin in aspic or concrete: at what point do we stop it becoming ruined any further? And at what point does that mean it isn't really a ruin at all? When does it become simply a memorial? Well, in this case, certainly by 1996, when the Atomic Bomb Dome was registered on the UNESCO World Heritage List, against not entirely unreasonable objections from both China and the United States.

* * *

The total number of war memorials in Britain is still being counted by various organisations, including the Imperial War Museum. A figure of sixty thousand seems likely, a staggering number, suggesting you can hardly walk down the street without encountering one, which is perhaps also to suggest they're so ubiquitous than it's easy to walk down the street and never see them at all.

London has about fourteen hundred of them, Sheffield has about two hundred and fifty, and though I would make some claims to know both these cities, I'd be hard pressed to think of a combined total of more than twenty, and that would include those ruined churches of St Dunstan-in-the-East and Christ Church Greyfriars in the City of London, as well as the war memorial that stands outside my old school in Sheffield.

As far as I know, none of the Sheffield memorials is exactly a ruin, though there is a wonderful memorial stone in Endcliffe Park, a chunk of rough, lichen-covered rock, with a couple of embedded metal plaques, commemorating an American Flying Fortress named Mi Amigo that crashed there in 1944. The plane, on a bombing mission against German targets in Denmark, was hit and struggled back into Allied territory, presumably heading for its base which was in Northampton, but it strayed off course and ended up over Sheffield. The precise details of the crash are likely to remain unresolved. One version has it that the pilot knew they were doomed and headed for the park simply to avoid crashing into nearby houses. Another version has it that he was simply hoping to do an emergency landing and survive, but as he was coming into land he saw children walking in the park, and deliberately slammed the plane into a nearby hillside to avoid killing them. Either way the entire crew of ten died in the crash.

This is just one of the many historical facts I never heard of growing up in Sheffield. For that matter, in all the many times I walked past and even went into the Sheffield City Hall, which is slap bang in the centre of town, and right across from the main war memorial, I never noticed that the Hall's stonework is absolutely pockmarked from a World War II bomb, just like St Paul's Cathedral. I suppose that wasn't the kind of ruin I was looking for when I went out walking the day I got my first 'serious' camera.

* * *

One of the pictures I took that day in Broomhill when I was a teenager is on the next page. I include it not because I think it's a very good picture of ruin (though I've seen plenty worse) but

because it leads to a couple of observations. The first is that this scene of dereliction was right beside one of the city's busy main roads, and yet there had been no attempt to fence it off and keep anyone out. I didn't have to climb over walls or barbed wire to get in; there wasn't even a No Trespassing sign. Anyone who wanted to walk in there could do so quite easily, and yet it appeared that few had, or if they had they'd left little trace. Maybe some of those windows were broken by vandals, but they'd also left a surprising number intact.

Which leads to the second observation, that these ruins were completely free of graffiti, a state of affairs that now seems unimaginable. We know that graffiti are an ancient and universal art form: there are some in the ruins of Pompeii, one of which, in the Basilica, reads, 'O walls, you have held up so much tedious graffiti that I am amazed you have not already collapsed in ruin.' 'Kilroy was here' graffiti appeared widely throughout the Second

World War; but until the late 1940s the art was practised without the benefit of spray paint in an aerosol can, which until then was unavailable to the general public. It's hard to imagine how graffiti art would have developed if the practitioners had had to continue to brush rather than spray. Certainly the term 'graffiti art' would have been meaningless to a citizen of Sheffield in the late 1960s, but tagging, by any other name, was familiar enough. I remember my mother being appalled when some lads painted their names (their real names, for all we knew) on the side of the local supermarket. She wasn't surprised that lads did this kind of thing, she just never expected it to happen in her own well-mannered neighbourhood. And of course that supermarket was not a ruin. Could it simply be that people had more respect for ruins back then?

Like any sane person I find some graffiti and street art just great and some just terrible, but I find it very interesting that in the book *Children of the Can*, by Felix Braun, Steve Wright and Richard Jones, a character named Turo, one of the first generation of Bristol street artists, describes the early work he and his crew did, and says, 'We were just basically destroying the city.' I find it even more interesting that when a graffiti artist decides to put up a lot of work in a very short time the process is known as bombing.

The other thing that occurs to me: if there *had* been any graffiti on those ruins in Broomhill I almost certainly wouldn't have photographed them; at that time they wouldn't have seemed like a suitable subject for a photograph at all, let alone 'serious' photography. How naïve I was. Today, books and websites featuring graffiti proliferate – again some great, some not. A parallel and frequently overlapping set of enthusiasts do the same for ruins, whether graffiti-covered or not. These ruin fans come in many kinds, art photographers of course, but also urban explorers and 'infiltrators', freakclimbers, exponents of parkour, war gamers, as well as the more orthodox history, war and archaeology buffs.

All this has led to a category of imagery known as Ruin Porn, a term that accuses the ruin enthusiast both of voyeurism and exploitation. Photographer Jason Oddy says:

> There is something distasteful about photographing ruins. Not so much ancient ruins, but modern ones. New ruins. It's exploitative – a way of aestheticising other people's misery. Worse it feels faintly pornographic, even necrophilic. Every time a new ruin pops up, hordes of so-called art photographers circle dumbly like vultures.

This is, of course, a charge that sticks rather better to rubber-necking tourists gawping at the devastation of Detroit or the aftermath of Katrina than it does to those who simply like poking around in World War II pillboxes or scrapyards. Still, I don't want to pretend I'm 'holier than they' in these matters: a ruin always involves a kind of human loss, whether of a home or a job or an environment. I think one has a duty to try to respond decently to that loss, not to belittle it, but who could claim to have absolutely always responded with the right amount of reverence and sympathy. John Ruskin had a lot to say about this, and I'll get to him later.

* * *

One person nobody could ever accuse of being a pornographer, a person who I imagine would faint clean away at the suggestion, is Marion Shoard who gave currency to the term 'edgelands'. Shoard, an environmentalist and now an advocate for old people's rights, used the word as the title of an essay first published in 2002, though reading it you could be forgiven for thinking it was written much earlier than that. Her 'edgelands' are those neglected zones, not quite country, not quite city, not quite suburb, though rubbing up against all these, sites where things are neglected, sometimes benignly, sometimes not, but in either case allowing certain things to come into being even as other things are falling apart. Personally I love to walk in these places, amid the decay and entropy, but I would also say that these edgelands are sometimes not literally on the edge of anything. Ruined, garbage-strewn wastelands can exist extremely close to supposedly pristine beauty spots: the shiny new supermarket sits right next to a row of boarded-up, smashed-up local shops.

Shoard writes, 'The apparently unplanned, certainly uncelebrated and largely incomprehensible territory where town and country meet rarely forms the setting for films, books or television shows.' Well, she apparently watches a very different set of movies and television shows. Has she never seen *The Sweeney*? Nor the *Fast and Furious* series? *Death Race*? Well, actually I suspect she hasn't. It gets worse.

She asks, 'How could we kindle more interest in the edgelands? Black-and-white photography, television, film, sculpture, painting and poetry could contribute much.' Black-and-white photography, eh? Oh come on, just how patronising and out of touch can you get? Is colour photography too vulgar for her? Is she not aware that the battle for colour photography as art was fought and won sometime round about 1975, not so long after I was taking my first faltering steps with my first 'serious' camera? Well, again, I suspect not.

In any case, she has a solution. 'Although one could argue that it is a contradiction to try to intrude the dead hand of the planner into something whose character is to be free, I none the less think that we should.' Oh, enough already. Obviously 'we' shouldn't, otherwise we – you – are trying to preserve something which is by definition unpreservable, which dies in the attempt at preservation. Finally Shoard offers the opinion, 'It is time for the edgelands to get the recognition that Emily Brontë and William Wordsworth brought to the moors and mountains and

John Betjeman to the suburbs.' I wonder if she's aware that for many people John Betjeman's best-known lines are likely to be 'Come friendly bombs and fall on Slough!' which of course they did just a few years after he'd written his poem in 1937, thereby creating ruins and indeed bomb-sites, although since the town had been used as a dumping ground for war surplus after World War I, and was packed with factories and trading estates, I'm sure it already had its edgelands.

Still, taking up Shoard's literary challenge, two poets, Paul Farley and Michael Symmons Roberts, who both grew up in the industrial or perhaps post-industrial north of England, wrote a terrific book titled *Edgelands*, a lyrical and only occasionally ironic, celebration of canals, allotments, landfills, retail parks, power stations and whatnot. By no means all of these things are ruins, though some definitely are; and in fact 'Ruins' is the title of one of the book's chapters, suggesting that ruin is a sub-category of edgeland, though I think you could equally make the case that edgelands are a sub-category of ruin.

Early in the book the authors deny that they're *flâneurs* or psychogeographers (a wise move, I'd say), but nevertheless their explorations do at least involve getting out of the car, walking around feeling the 'specific effects of the geographical environment', as recommended by Guy Debord, and drifting about among the long grass, rubble and broken glass. They write, 'To walk in edgeland ruins is to feel absence and presence at the same time.' They get into a disused bank in Cardiff: . . . 'pens still clung to chains on counters approached on all sides by damp and mould. On the other side of the counters . . . a sign says: "Smile. Say 'Good Morning/Afternoon'. Say 'How can I help you, Sir/Madam?' " Why do these courtesies seem to be mocked now, by the smashed windows and rotten floorboards? Didn't they know that at some point their bank would come to ruin?' Well, maybe they did, maybe they didn't. But so what if they did? How would this actually have affected the 'courtesies' they offered to their customers? The world may be falling into ruin, but that's no reason to be rude, is it? But that passage did make me recall something from my own past that I'd completely forgotten.

The first full-time job I ever had was in the tax office in Sheffield. Very uncool, I know: a long and not very interesting story, a dodgy uncle was involved. In the office I did whatever menial tasks came my way, but essentially I was a filing clerk, putting an apparently infinite number of pieces of paper into alphabetical order. It was by no means the worst or hardest job you could have, but it was mind-numbing, and at the end of the day I went home with my brain twanging, still putting the world into order, alphabetising the street names I saw, the destinations on the front of buses, the words in newspaper headlines. The process went on even when I got into bed and tried to sleep.

My method of stilling this barely assuagable urge to put the world in order, was to imagine myself alone in the tax office at night, running through corridors, offices and back rooms, tipping over trays of deduction cards, pulling files off shelves, knocking over desks, cabinets, smashing light fittings, throwing chairs through windows, until I'd reimagined the entire tax office, disordered, in chaos, functionally destroyed, trashed; just like that bank in Cardiff. Only when I had ruined the place could I get a good night's sleep.

* * *

I wish Rose Macaulay had been alive to give us her opinion of edgelands; the places rather than the essay or book. Macaulay, to my mind the Ruin Queen, is the author of *Pleasure of Ruins*, which could be a holy text for ruin enthusiasts, though I don't imagine that many 'urban explorers' keep a copy in their back-pack. The book was first published in 1953, and there have been many editions, including a 'photographic interpretation' by Roloff Beny with a severely abridged text. There are very, very few people in Beny's photographs, and only one unambiguously shows anybody walking. Macaulay's original consisted of 450 or so pages of dense text, with just a few very small, mostly non-photographic, black and white plates as illustrations.

Macaulay's title is an odd one, isn't it? Why not *the* pleasure and why only a single pleasure? Isn't there more than one? Be that as it may, the book is wonderfully strange, eccentric and opinionated, encyclopaedic, highly literate and literary, and Macaulay conveys a genuine passion and enthusiasm for ruins, even as she wrestles with defining exactly what the pleasure is.

Macaulay was a great traveller, but she was prepared to discuss sites she'd never been to. Here, quite untroubled by what we would today call political correctness, she describes the ruined cities and temples of Cambodia, 'According to travellers, one comes on them like truffles in a wood, seductively decaying in green boscage, to be dug up and plucked by any white explorers who happen along.' Well yes, there is maybe more than one reason why urban explorers don't keep a copy in their backpack.

On the first page of the book she says, 'It is pretty safe to suppose that the earliest ruin pleasure was inextricably mixed with triumph over enemies, with moral judgement and vengeance, and with the violent excitements of war.' 'Excitements' is just great, isn't it? She knew what she was talking about. She'd lived through the London Blitz, and seen her own flat utterly destroyed. She was sixty years old at the time, and therefore over seventy when *Pleasure of Ruins* was published, a time when she might reasonably have been expected to take the long view, and indeed she does. In a chapter titled 'The Stupendous Past' she writes about Roman ruins and what we do when we view them:

> Thus pleasure-seeking in the theatres, repairing the broken bridges, even, perhaps, running water along the aqueducts, thus we link the stupendous past with our smothering,

runagate, unlovely present, appeasing our eternally nostalgic appetite with its desperate reaches beyond the horizon to where stretch the limitless, only partly charted, dimly seen and largely obliviated civilities and deserts of time.

Well, we wouldn't put it quite that way, but she's dead right, isn't she? Ruins make us look forward as well as back. We see the past in ruins and restore it in our imagination. We see our own present, and imagine how it will be when it lies in ruin. Both are melancholy pleasures to be sure, but pleasures nevertheless, even if beset by *Ruinenschmerz*, a word that's Macaulay's own invention as far as I can tell.

I love Rose Macaulay's book. In quite a different way I love the book and website *Derelict London* in which Paul Talling so obsessively photographs and catalogues the shuttered pubs, abandoned sports fields and wrecked cars of London. I love the ruin photographs of John Divola, Richard Misrach, Richard Mosse. I like watching movies that feature ruin: Rosselini's *Rome Open City*, Richard Lester's *The Bed Sitting Room*, Peter Greenaway's *The Belly of an Architect*, Herzog's *Fata Morgana* and *Lessons of Darkness*. I like seeing art inspired by ruin: Piranesi's real and imaginary ruins, Anselm Kiefer and his 'world of ruination'. I love the Japanese noise band Ruins, whose music evokes destruction and chaos just as much as the name does.

But reading and looking and listening are only part of it. Above all what I really like to do is *walk* in ruins. And if, like me, you have some reputation as a walker, and if you tell people that you're writing a book about walking in ruins, some get it and some don't, but a surprising number of both groups tend ask you, 'Well, what's your favourite ruin walk?' Again I want to give a reasonable reply, and I definitely don't want to be evasive or pretentious or precious, so I say, 'Stonehenge.' It's not absolutely true, but it generally shuts them up.

2

Some Scenes from the Life of a Ruin Walker

> It is the familiar tragedy of archaeology – the sacrifice of beauty to knowledge. Burckhardt wept over it on revisiting the demossed Greek temples of Sicily after twenty years; Augustus Hare over Hadrian's cleaned-up villa . . . Robert Byron, looking on Persepolis . . . found . . . the cold, shining grey stone repellent and like an aluminium saucepan.
>
> Rose Macaulay, *Pleasure of Ruins*

Stoned henges

Henry of Huntingdon (who died circa 1154) considered Stonehenge one of the four wonders of England. No Roman or Saxon historian mentioned it at all, nevertheless Inigo Jones decided it was probably a Roman Temple, and in the late nineteenth century the architectural historian James Fergusson claimed it was a Saxon selpuchre. This was only marginally more probable than the theory propagated in the seventeenth century by Edmund Bolton, historian and poet, that it was the memorial tomb of Boudicca. John Aubrey also in the seventeenth century, and then William Stukeley in the eighteenth, were convinced it was a Druids' temple.

By the twentieth century Erik Von Däniken was claiming its size and scope was so great that it must have been built by aliens, just as nine centuries earlier Geoffrey of Monmouth had thought, for similar reasons, that it must have been magicked up by Merlin. Many quite reasonable people still see it as a spiritual vortex, and I have found at least one source that considers it a 'transdimensional portal'. Between 1972 and 1985 it was the site of the Summer Solstice Free Festival, a brief tradition that ended in 1985 in a 'police riot', remembered now as the Battle of the Beanfield.

Replicas and reinterpretations of Stonehenge abound. Street artist Banksy did his own interpretation using graffiti-painted portaloos at Glastonbury. A bouncy replica created by the artist Jeremy Deller appeared in London as part of the 2012 Olympics. In Maryhill, in Washington State, there's a full size, concrete version, looking the way it might have looked before it fell into ruin. This one was built immediately after the First World War by a Quaker businessman named Samuel Hill. Hill believed that the actual Stonehenge had been the site of human sacrifice – William Blake, among many others, thought the same – and this new version was to symbolise the fact that although we were no longer 'uncivilised' like the Druids of Stonehenge, we nevertheless still sacrificed men to the great god of war. Today it's part of an art museum.

Carhenge, in Nebraska, is a recreation of Stonehenge in its current ruined state, but built using cars instead of stones. I once saw a model somebody had built in their front yard in Hackney using breeze blocks. A seriously and comically undersised version appears in the movie *Spinal Tap*, and I have an even smaller model of it sitting right beside my desk: 'Build Your Own Ancient Wonder' it says on the box. As the archaeologist Jaquetta Hawkes put it, 'Every age gets the Stonehenge it deserves' – the great British Ur-ruin.

Dr Samuel Johnson probably would not have been impressed by any of this. Boswell describes, in *A Journal of a Tour to the Hebrides*, trying to interest Johnson in a Druids' temple, a few miles outside Inverness, a fine example with two full double circles of standing stones, but Johnson declined to visit. He had already seen a ruined version in Strichen, in Aberdeenshire, and now declared, 'To go and see one druidical temple is only to see that it is nothing, for there is neither art nor power in it; and seeing one is quite enough.'

Julian Cope, author of *The Modern Antiquarian* and all-round enthusiast for ancient sites and stones, might have had a small amount of sympathy. In the TV series based on his book he describes his first encounter with Stonehenge:

> I came out of punk, and punk was taught to sort of diss everything to do with hippies, and Stonehenge was to do with hippies, so I was one of those who came to mock and remained to pray. You know I went to Stonehenge this one day with my mother-in-law and she said ,'Darling, when was this done?' And I told her the date, I said it was about two thousand years before Christ. 'Wow that's just amazing. It's physically so impressive.' And I thought wow and I suddenly saw it through her eyes, and I was suddenly impressed by it.

Cope and his mother-in-law are absolutely right. Stonehenge really is genuinely impressive: the idea no less than the reality. It's ancient of course, and that does count for something in a ruin. Scholars argue about the date, but the consensus is that some parts are even older than Cope says, more like three thousand years BC. But what really impresses is that, quite simply, it looks magnificent in its ruined state: simple, serious, primal. Those massive uprights and crossbeams (sarsens and lintels to be precise), those freestanding monoliths in the centre (bluestones), have a scale and a solidity, a visual and atavistic power that simply won't be denied. There are plenty of artists' impressions to help us visualise it in its unruined state, though there is a minority view that the structure was never completed at all and was always a kind of ruin, or at least an abandoned project.

Adding to the appeal is the fact that we still don't really know what Stonehenge was, what it did, what it was for. We certainly don't know for sure how it was built or how some of the stone got there from Wales. Modern historians are thoroughly convinced that it was never used by ancient Druids, though it is used by modern ones. Very possibly it was a burial ground – a necropolis – and possibly a place of healing, where people came in search of a miracle, but we can't be sure. Many of the excavated graves have contained bodies of the deformed and the mutilated, though it's easy enough to think of other explanations for their presence.

And yes, sure, Stonehenge works as an astrological calendar, and kind of observatory, but the reasons why our ancestors would need a calendar or observatory of such massive size, constructed with such immense difficulty, over such a long period of time, remains obscure. I can't help wondering wither some Bronze Age types built it as a work of art, a precursor to Robert Smithson's *Spiral Jetty*, but I seem to be alone in that theory, and of course I have absolutely no evidence. In any case, I think these myriad uncertainties are part of the appeal of Stonehenge. All ruins are mysterious to a degree, and here, despite all the research and excavations, the various theories and 'decodings', the mystery seems satisfyingly insoluble. It's absolutely what we want in a ruin, but it may not be *all* we want.

* * *

If any of the visitors to Stonehenge were experiencing the effects of a spiritual vortex when I was there, they were doing a great job of disguising it. New Agers and countercultural types were entirely absent. The ones I saw looked like just plain folks of the international tourist class; the audio tour was available in ten languages.

A fair percentage of visitors were there as part of a coach tour. I heard one of the guides telling his charges that they had forty minutes to see the ruins, visit the toilet and gift shop, and be back on the bus. These days you approach Stonehenge through a subway so that the car park and all the ancillary buildings are on the other side of the road, the A344, and the thing itself stands alone, separate, in the middle of a large, sloping grassy expanse. This is a very good thing. You see Stonehenge from a distance, whole, isolated exactly as you imagined it. You admire the shape, the size, the impact, and only then do you approach it.

Gone are the days when you could easily get up close and personal with the stones. Back in the nineteenth century visitors could hire hammers from a blacksmith in Avebury, two miles away, and chip off chunks of stone to take home as souvenirs. Earlier generations had removed stone to use as building material, a common enough practice with ruins, from the Pyramids to Hadrian's Wall. Now it's run by English Heritage, and kept safe from harm, although back in 2008 a couple of chancers defied the ban and climbed in at night and chipped off a coin-sized piece from the Heel Stone, a monolith outside the main circle, right up against the boundary fence, an easy target and quite a temptation to anyone with a hammer, I'd say. Security guards spotted the culprits and chased them off before they did more serious damage, but they were never caught. Some Wiltshire lad may be displaying a fragment of Stonehenge in his cabinet of curiosities even now.

There are various times at which you're still able to walk among the stones themselves: sunset tours, the occasional art- or solstice-related event, but I opted for the standard 'pay your money and in you go' daytime visit. In one, strictly limited sense, the bus driver was right, forty minutes might be enough time to 'see' Stonehenge. It would be more than enough time to walk one circuit of the irregularly shaped path that loops around the henge. You could do it in about ten minutes if you really wanted to. This loop, according to my wrist-mounted GPS, was exactly .33 miles and I couldn't help thinking there might be something

deliberate and numerologically significant in that, but I didn't find anybody to ask about it.

The path kept us at a safe distance; the safety of the stones being far more of an issue than the safety of visitors. At the closest point the path was perhaps twenty feet away from the stones, while at other times it was maybe a hundred yards away. It's extremely hard to see Stonehenge with new eyes. It's so recognisable, we've seen it depicted so often, and it looks so much like itself. And maybe that was why nobody seemed to be really looking at it. Some were taking pictures of the stones, of course, including me, which is always a great way of not seeing, but rather more were photographing each other and in some cases themselves while standing immobile on the path with their backs to Stonehenge, using it as a backdrop. This also made progress rather tricky for the more committed walker.

I never quite understand why people want to be photographed in front of landmarks. I suppose it must be a kind of proof that they were really there, but I'm never sure who needs this proof. Is it for friends and family who might otherwise think you were lying when you said you'd walked around Stonehenge? Or do people need the proof for their own benefit, because otherwise they can't really believe they've been there?

Either way this seemed an essentially unsophisticated, to say nothing of uncosmic, response to the ruins. And when I saw a Buddhist monk in full rig, wearing the saffron robes and some rather nifty footwear that looked like a cross between socks and tea-cosies, I thought right, I'll watch this guy, he'll be different, he must surely be here to tune in to some kind of spiritual energy. He promptly approached a stranger, handed him a camera and mimed that he wanted to have his picture taken in front of the henge.

I'm still not sure if this was better or worse than the one person I saw who actually looked as though he might be having some kind of deeper experience. He was a dapper, distinguished, grey-haired, grey-bearded Japanese man, who stood still and alone on the grass, some way off the walking path, and even farther from Stonehenge, but he peered at it through half-closed eyes, apparently drifting into a meditative state. I was simultaneously impressed and sceptical. He looked the part, but how could you be sure it was genuine? Maybe he was trying to perform some quiet, discreet ritual, but wasn't he being way too exhibitionistic about it?

Impressed as I was by the look of Stonehenge, I didn't feel any cosmic vibe, either discreetly or exhibitionistically. My experience was as 'materialist' as anyone else's, and perhaps worse, since I found I was spending more time looking at the people who were looking at Stonehenge than I was looking at Stonehenge itself. People-watching is an honourable activity, but it's not why you go to Stonehenge. I decided I should do some *walking*, cover some ground, try to see the stones from all angles.

But here's an odd, if ultimately obvious, thing. It's very hard indeed to walk a circular route while keeping your eye on what's in the centre of the circle. Unless you walk sideways, or walk with your head turned at ninety degrees to your body (which is not recommended at Stonehenge since you'd walk straight into somebody taking a picture of themselves), you're going to have to stop and start, pause to look, move on, look again. If you look strictly where you're going, you're always bound to be looking away from the centre. So a walk around Stonehenge involves walking and stopping, turning and looking, walking some more, looking from a different angle, walking on, stopping again, and so forth.

Or you could, of course, just put your head down, ignore the ruins, do your best to ignore the other people, and simply walk. That's what I found myself doing, sometimes on the path, sometimes on the grassy field. In no time I'd done half a dozen circuits, and in fact I could see the ruins out of the corner of my eye most of the time, even when I wasn't looking directly at them, and for a while this felt good and interestingly perverse. It was a different way of engaging with the ruins. But then it seemed utterly absurd. If I hadn't come to Stonehenge to people-watch, even less had I come to do laps.

For what it's worth, I didn't see anyone else make more than one circuit of the looped path, though no doubt some people must. But I did hear a South African couple discussing where their friend Bob had got to. 'Maybe he's gone to do another turn,' the man said laughing, as if this were the most improbable and hilarious thing he could imagine.

But in this process of mine I did notice a couple of things. First, how without any conspicuous security presence, and with a minimum of Keep Out signs, everyone was extraordinarily well behaved and well ordered. They were all positively serene. Nobody was running around, nobody was yelling. Nobody hopped over the extremely low rope to get a closer look or a touch, though they easily could have. What were the authorities going to do to you? Throw you out of the field? Call the cops? Well yes, possibly they were. But I'd have thought you could say, 'Sorry, officer, I couldn't help it. I was pulled by the spiritual vortex,' and that would have been defence enough, surely.

For that matter, despite the fact that there were no signs saying that the path was a one-way route, everybody went the same way, without even thinking about it. You'd have thought somebody would have felt the urge to go against the flow but nobody did, not even me. And this was why I was able to notice the second thing. When you looked up from a low area on the north-east side of the path you could see Stonehenge rising above you on the higher ground. And you also saw a procession of people on either side of it, outlined against the sky, some moving towards it from the right, some moving away from it on the left. They were not in single file and not moving as a unit, but all moved at more or less the same pace, and all in the same direction. My first thought was that it looked like a dance of death, but in fact it was more stately and deliberate than that.

Had you been up close you'd have seen these walkers taking pictures, heard them talking on cell phones, discussing what they were having for lunch, but from the right distance they looked like they were on a serious and solemn walking pilgrimage, and I suppose it is just conceivable, if a little unlikely, that one or two of them actually were. My feeling then and now is that Stonehenge is a great ruin, but it doesn't offer a great walk.

* * *

You'll find plenty of people who think that Stonehenge has been completely spoiled, both by the sheer number of visitors, and the fact that visitors are kept at such a distance from the stones. One recommendation is simply to head for the stones at Avebury, a site that is less touristy for sure (though not entirely *untouristy*), though also a good deal less grand and impressive.

My own favourite stone circle, largely because it's the first one I ever saw, is the Nine Ladies on Stanton Moor, in Derbyshire. This is modest in the extreme: nine rather formless lumps of millstone grit, none of them more than three feet high. I always thought it was safe from being spoiled by tourism because it was so unspectacular, but then some commercial interests fought a bitter campaign some years back to reopen a couple of quarries in the area. They didn't get their way. Local conservationists asserted, rightly enough, that quarrying would have spoiled the environment containing the ruins, and the ruins took precedence. This was a significant victory, but it does raise the question of ruining a ruin.

For a decade or more I carried in my head a wonderfully pleasing image of the ruined leper hospital at Dunwich, on the Suffolk coast, dating from the thirteenth century and probably a chapel before it was a hospital. Dunwich is a fine place to walk, a locus of fabulous ruin: there's a ruined abbey, there's a whole ruined village under the sea just off the coast, but it was the leper hospital that really moved me. It was small, but lofty, made from Caen limestone, some of it with rough but intricate carvings. When I first saw it there was no roof, no glass in the windows, parts of the walls were missing, ivy was strangling the masonry, long grass grew up through some irregular stone slabs on the ground: bare, ruined choirs indeed. It was ancient, Gothic, not exactly threatening but a very long way from comforting; and one thought of those poor lepers, outside the town, sick, exiled, essentially incarcerated; human ruins.

Of course I knew that there was nothing fixed about the particular condition of ruin of the old hospital; it obviously hadn't always been like this, might not even have been like this for very long at all. Some maintenance had clearly been done: it hadn't been left to fall into absolute decay, dissolution hadn't been allowed to win completely, but the balance between nature and structure, between neglect and preservation seemed just about perfect. It was a glorious but, I now know, transitory state of affairs.

Last time I went back it had been all been cleaned up, tidied up. They (and I'm not absolutely sure quite who 'they' were) had decided the structure was dangerous; repointing had been done, the ivy had been hacked back, turf put down, there was a park bench, there was even a wrought-iron fence and a gate, which could be locked to keep out the riff-raff. I could see the point to some extent: you don't want people going in there tagging, having bonfires or dogging parties or whatever they get up to on the Suffolk coast these days. That would certainly spoil the ruins. But there was no indication that any of that had been happening anyway. These 'improvements' seemed to have been done in the spirit of beautification, which meant that the ruin was spoiled in a quite different way. It wasn't simply preserved or stabilised, it was *tarted up*. It had lost its charm, and its capacity to stir the imagination. Oh yes, a ruin can be ruined.

Valking with Werner

I've long known, and in fact have often quoted, a line from Werner Herzog: 'Tourism is sin, and travel on foot virtue.' I even mentioned it in my previous book *The Lost Art of Walking* in relation to his memoir *Of Walking in Ice.* I've always thought it was a pretty good line, or maybe a pretty good joke, and I did know that it came from something called the 'Minnesota Declaration', but I'd never stopped to wonder why Herzog was making a declaration – he doesn't seem the kind of movie director who goes in for manifestos – and I'd certainly never thought to question what Minnesota had to do with it.

I now know that it wasn't so much a manifesto as a text to accompany a screening of *Lessons of Darkness*, his 1992 movie, shot in Kuwait, after the First Gulf War (though neither place nor event is named in the movie), showing the ruined oilfields, ruined cities, ruined forests, some of them still in flames. It's a documentary framed as a science-fiction movie, and it really doesn't have much walking in it, since much of the footage is shot from helicopters. But the opening scene does show a man on foot, a man reduced to a black silhouette with an orange inferno raging behind him. He's wearing a hard hat and, I take it, a flameproof suit. Herzog's voice-over, using the science-fiction conceit, says of this man, 'The first creature we encountered tried to communicate something to us' – and the man is indeed waving his arms, stomping his foot, trying to convey something or other. I had always assumed he was signalling to the cameraman, who must also have been on foot at this stage, to stop filming and get the hell out of there, but the production notes that come with the DVD say the 'creature' is a fireman signalling to somebody to turn off the water. I'm sure Herzog would allow me my own interpretation.

I also now know that the screening which inspired the

Minnesota Declaration took place at the Walker (yes, really) Art Center in Minneapolis, Minnesota on 30 April 1999. The Walker is a fabulously well-endowed museum, and it has a huge sculpture garden attached, a place in which I went walking when I happened to be in Minneapolis, tagging along on my wife's business trip. While she did business, I mooched aimlessly around the city, alone.

I realised I'd done rather a lot of this kind of thing in my life. When I was young I could never find people to travel with. It wasn't that I had no friends, but the friends I had were a stay-at-home bunch. I always ended up travelling by myself, because otherwise I wouldn't have travelled at all. This resulted in a lot of walking alone in strange cities. And, naturally, I sometimes felt lonely and bereft, and I often headed for museums and art galleries, because they were places where I felt less alone. And sometimes I headed for ruins: in Athens or on the Greek islands. All these were tourist attractions no doubt. Of course I wasn't really alone in Minneapolis. I knew I'd be meeting up with my wife at the end of the day, but even so, the elements of loneliness that I'd experienced as a solitary young man came oozing back. I walked through the sculpture garden looking at all big-name art, works by Claes Oldenburg, Henry Moore, Richard Serra, Tony Cragg, Isamu Noguchi, among them, and I felt profoundly, not quite explicably, melancholy.

To the extent that I was a tourist I was no doubt, in Herzog's terms, a sinner; to the extent that I was on foot I hope I was virtuous. It was a weekday and the sculpture garden wasn't crowded, though there were quite a few parents and children. We were all 'walking' in some sense, but it was the kind of walking that people do when in the presence of art: halting, respectful, attentive, solemn. Some of the parents were doing their best to make their kids understand they were in a sculpture garden rather than a playground. There were mixed results, obviously.

I found a quiet, unflashy piece of sculpture, deep in the shadows and easy to miss. It was a life-size bronze of a middle-aged man in a raincoat: he looked a little like Nabokov. The raincoat would have made him overdressed for the day I was there – the temperature was in the eighties – although I'm sure he'd have been underdressed for a real, punishing Minneapolis winter. I wouldn't say that he was ruined, but he was certainly weatherbeaten, the surface of the bronze had acquired a beautiful patina: this was a man who'd been out in the elements for a good long time. He looked not so much melancholy as downright miserable.

A mother and her little boy were standing beside me as I looked at the sculpture. The child turned to his mother and said, referring to the sculpture, not to me, though that wasn't clear at first, 'Do we know that man?' His mother assured him that no, 'we' didn't know this man, and that seemed to be explanation enough for the kid, though I'd have thought that answer would have raised other questions in the kid's mind: if we didn't know him then why had somebody bothered to make a sculpture of him?

The sculpture was 'Walking Man' by George Segal, from 1988. The Walker Art Center website tells me, 'This solitary figure captures an overwhelming sense of the isolation one can encounter in contemporary society', which strikes me as a bit overdeterministic but yes, there is something moving about the man's isolation, his quiet hopelessness, further emphasised by the fact that this is a walking man who isn't moving, who isn't ever going anywhere. He's frozen, staying exactly where he is, while the rest of the world walks past, not knowing who he is, in many cases not even noticing him.

* * *

I wasn't specifically seeking out ruin as I walked around Minneapolis, but I didn't doubt that I'd find some one way or another, because I always do, and this process was made much simpler in the event by the existence of the Mill Ruins Park, on the south-west bank of the Mississippi River.

Like many a city with a great but faded industrial past, Minneapolis has attempted revitalisation by turning the remnants of that past into tourist attractions. At the end of the nineteenth century the city thrived around the Mississippi, and especially around the St Anthony Falls, harnessing water power mostly for use in various kinds of mill, including paper, wool, cotton, lumber and, most importantly of all, flour. Minneapolis became a world centre for flour milling, and got the nickname Mill City. That was a long time ago and it's all over now, though Minneapolis remains a thriving and prosperous city

The ruins referred to in the name of the riverside park come in several forms: there are some old foundations down at water level that look like the remains of an archaeological dig; there are certain mills and silos that are no longer in use but are still intact; and there's one giant, magnificent ruin, as grand and impressive as an English castle, the remains of the Washburn A mill, many storeys high, roofless, the elegant stone walls broken and pierced. All around the area are neatly-laid-out walking paths and bike trails; the Stone Arch Bridge, which crosses the river and once served the railways, is now fully open to pedestrians. My impression was that these paths were being used more by locals than by bona fide tourists, but even so, I'm sure Werner Herzog would have disapproved.

What's left of the Washburn A Mill also contains the Mill City Museum which bills itself as the 'most explosive museum in the world'. The reason: flour production seems to have been just as dangerous as other, apparently more threatening and heavier, industrial processes. Flour dust, it turns out, is highly inflammable and a stray spark in the mill on the evening of 2 May 1878 ignited some of that flour dust, causing an explosion

that blew the roof off the Washburn A Mill and effectively demolished it, as well as destroying two adjacent mills. The resulting fire also destroyed a third of the Minneapolis business district.

But that is only tangentially relevant to the ruin you currently see when you're standing on the banks of the Mississippi, looking at the Mill City Museum. This is a different ruin. The mill was rebuilt after the explosion, and was in business till 1965, when it shut down because it was no longer profitable; and it stood there, unused but solid, until 1991, when a massive, unexplained fire (homeless squatters trying to keep warm is a reasonable bet) destroyed the rebuilt mill. A decade later these ruins were stabilised and cleaned up, and restored to their current level of ruin, keeping turbine pits, train tracks, and some ancillary railway buildings for display purposes, and they became a home for the museum.

This is a formidable ruin, majestic, picturesque, an industrial archetype, but looking at it you might be reminded of another part of Werner Herzog's 'Minnesota Declaration'. Here he's defending *Lessons of Darkness* from the charge that it might not be telling the literal truth. He takes a shot at more prosaic documentarians and says, 'Filmmakers of *cinéma vérité* resemble tourists who take pictures amid ancient ruins of facts.' The mills of Minneapolis aren't ancient, but they're much photographed, and I agree that taking pictures of well-tended, 'revitalised' ruins in a postindustrial theme park is hardly the stuff of great art, much less of (Herzog's term) ecstatic truth.

Up on a high floor of the mill, when you've been through the museum, you can step out on to a rooftop, an observation deck, and then look across the river, beyond the Stone Arch Bridge, and see another fine building: looking more like a collection of buildings, this is the old Pillsbury Flour Mill, not an obvious ruin when seen from that distance, though I was told it was no longer in business. Its aspect is thoroughly sculptural: big masses, a giant structure made up of diverse but harmonious architectural parts; the design is credited to one Leroy S. Buffington. There are slabs, cylinders, cubes and arches, making it more like a whole city block than a single structure; it is part office building, part factory, with a row of silos forming what looks like a wing off to one side and a water tank sitting conspicuously atop part of the roof. Some of the buildings are stone, some industrial tile, and those silos are a gleaming white-painted concrete. And up on the very top, in what had to be a gigantic script in order to be so clearly visible from so far away, were free-standing letters spelling out 'Pillsbury's Best Flour'. I knew I had to walk to it.

There weren't many people in the Mill Ruins Park that day, and only one or two were walking across the Stone Arch Bridge, and by the time I got to the other side of the river I was all alone and felt like I was in a small, still, silent, no man's land. The Pillsbury building loomed larger than ever from here, but now it looked far less unified, less like something designed to be looked at. It presented a façade to the world across the river, but here you could see into the workings. It wasn't a row of buildings but a whole conglomeration, built around a broad central space. What had looked like a wing of silos from afar was actually a massive row of them a few hundred yards long, stretching all the way behind the other buildings. In that central space, wide as a street, there were defunct railway lines running through the concrete floor, thick grass pushing up through the cracks. And here the architecture was much less grand: there was bare concrete, rusted sheet metal, catwalks, pipes, bunker-like kiosks made of breeze blocks.

There was a chain-link fence that clearly hadn't kept out graffiti sprayers, since their work and its aftermath were clearly visible. In any case, one edge of the fence had been opened up, perhaps cut, and pushed back so that even a less than reckless man, such as myself, could get in there and get closer, without doing any damage. For what it's worth, this is pretty much my rule on exploring ruins. I'll ignore Keep Out and No Trespassing signs. I'll hop over a fence or a wall, go in through an open window or door, but I won't cut fences, break windows or smash down doors. I'm sure this makes me a wimp in the eyes of the urban infiltration 'community', but I reckon it might one day persuade a cop or even a judge to cut me some slack. The fact is, I don't want to be chased by security guards or dogs, and there were none around that day at the Pillsbury site. So I squeezed through the gap in the fence and walked into the centre of that broad, high-sided open space, treading on broken glass and stray boards, admiring the convoluted, windowless shapes and industrial textures all around me. It was like walking into a silent, abandoned city. It was wonderful.

I couldn't find any open doors or windows, and it didn't matter much. I was happy enough to stay outside. This was pretty much everything I've ever looked for in a ruin: substantial, elegant, a little bit Bauhaus, a little bit threatening, a little bit ghostly, clearly not conceived of as a 'fun' building, though to my eyes it had something playful and joyous about it. I walked around in a mild fugue state until I saw a sign telling me that this whole edifice was about to become a loft-style development of a thousand or so apartments, though I couldn't see that any work was actually being done at that time. I had some seriously mixed feelings about this proposed repurposing. A great ruin would disappear. That was a shame, a very bad thing. But I consoled myself with the thought that this made my visit all the more special. I was experiencing something crucial, something that goes along with seeing so many ruins, that in retrospect had definitely applied to the ruined leper hospital in Dunwich: the realisation that ruin is so often a temporary state of affairs. You see ruins on a specific day, at a specific moment in your and their life. They didn't used to look like this; they won't look exactly like this for very long: few things stay the same, some things change out of all recognition, and maybe that's a good thing after all. Visit Stonehenge, or the Mill City Museum for that matter, and you pretty much know what you're going to get: a ruin that has achieved a certain finished form, and you also know that a great deal of work is being done to maintain that form. Visit a ruin in transition or neglect and you have something personal, something that's all yours.

The penultimate item in Werner Herzog's 'Minnesota Declaration' runs as follows: 'Life in the oceans must be sheer hell. A vast, merciless hell of permanent and immediate danger. So much of a hell that during evolution some species – including man – crawled, fled onto some small continents of solid land, where the *Lessons of Darkness* continue.' I suppose a man has to learn to crawl in the ruins before he can learn to walk in them.

Strolling with Speer: The Military-Industrial Ridiculous

If you believe Albert Speer's memoir *Inside the Third Reich* (and you could be forgiven if you didn't completely), you may also believe that he and Hitler shared certain opinions about ruins. He tells us that in early 1934 Hitler invited him to design a permanent stone grandstand to replace the temporary seating at Zeppelin Field in Nuremberg, one of the Nazi rally grounds.

It was Speer's first major commission and he wanted to impress. He worked hard, struggled with it, and finally came up with a grand design, far beyond his brief. It was a grandstand thirteen hundred feet long and eighty feet high, based on the Pergamon Altar, a second-century-BC temple dedicated to Zeus. That altar was built in Asia Minor, discovered by German archaeologists, excavated, then transported to Berlin at the beginning of the twentieth century where it's still on display today in the Pergamon Museum. Speer claimed his design was 'almost twice the length of the Baths of Caracalla in Rome'. The classical references are no surprise, but it's curiously significant that those Caracalla baths were built by prisoners of war, and one of the war crimes for which Speer was convicted was the employment of slave labour in Germany's wartime munitions factories.

Speer admitted to having had some trepidation when he showed his design to Hitler, but the Führer examined the plans and the plaster model Speer had made, and he approved. He said, 'Agreed,' and Speer was in business. Hitler, said Speer, believed that architecture should transmit the spirit of its time to future generations. Nations were bound to have 'periods of weakness' but the presence of noble, ancient architectural ruins would remind citizens of what their civilisation had once been and what it might be again. Mussolini's Italy, for example, was in the doldrums at that time, but at least the Italians had the ruins of ancient Rome to spur them on to greatness. What did Germany have?

Well one thing they had, right there next to Zeppelin Field, was the ruin of a former streetcar depot, demolished some time earlier, but never entirely cleared away. What remained was an ignoble and uninspiring heap of broken concrete and rusting iron, a 'dreary sight' according to Speer, obviously not the way any civilisation would wish to be remembered by posterity, nor the kind of ruin that was likely to inspire any greatness in the future.

And so Speer came up with 'A Theory of Ruin Value' (in German *Ruinenwert*). The idea, simply, was that architecture should be built with an eye to the future. Buildings should be constructed bearing in mind that one day they would lie in ruins. 'By using special materials and by applying certain principles of statistics, we should be able to build structures which even in a state of decay, after hundreds or (such were our reckonings) thousands of years, would more or less resemble Roman models.' Speer made a 'Romantic drawing' for Hitler, showing how his Zeppelin Field grandstand would look with its masonry crumbling, its fallen columns covered in ivy. Hitler liked it a lot.

Speer, like anyone, could see there was, at the very least, a paradox here. If the Third Reich was going to last a thousand years wasn't it irrelevant and even blasphemous to imagine it in ruins? Some in Hitler's entourage apparently thought so, but Hitler (according to Speer) was all in favour of ruin value, finding the ideas 'logical and illuminating'. Speer wrote, 'He gave orders that in the future the important buildings of his Reich were to be erected in keeping with the principles of this "law of ruins".' The transition from theory to law had been a remarkably swift one.

What to make of this? In the first place, Speer was surely right to be worried about showing his design to Hitler. If you're asked to design some raked seating and you come up with a massive, faux-classical temple, a client far more even-tempered than Adolf Hitler might think you were getting a little above yourself. One explanation may simply be that Speer knew his man, and that man's megalomania. He was flattering Hitler by suggesting that the rally grounds should be as magnificent as the buildings of the ancient world: nothing was too good for the Nazi Party. At the same time he was also flattering himself and his own powers too: his buildings would be as great as those of ancient Rome.

As for whether Hitler really accepted Speer's notion of ruin value, and especially whether he would, for a moment, have taken any pleasure in imagining the future destruction of the buildings of the Reich, I seriously doubt; though by the time *Inside the Third Reich* was published the Führer was in no position to challenge Speer's version. One possible explanation for Speer's insisting that Hitler approved of his idea was that Speer was trying to demonstrate in his memoir that Hitler at that time was still a rational man, and that therefore it wasn't unreasonable for an architect to want to work for him. Proof of Hitler's rationality, in Speer's account, was that they shared the same views when it came to architecture and ruins.

Speer and Hitler would eventually have opposing views on

the value of ruin, at least in so far as it applied to Hitler's 'scorched earth' policy, the Nero Decree, to leave nothing standing either in Germany or the occupied territories as German troops retreated. Speer by then was Minister of Armaments and War Production, and felt able to resist Hitler's orders. Perhaps he thought it was one thing to create a building that would look good in a ruined state, quite another to ruin a whole country.

* * *

Hitler's concern with ruins was always some way from being merely aesthetic, although in his role as an amateur painter he had once found ruins a suitable subject. The painting opposite, titled *Ruins of a Cloister in Messines*, was done in 1914. The church had been ruined in battle, by the invading Germans. Hitler probably painted it from life. The crypt of the church was being used as a field hospital and he was treated there as an injured corporal in the German army. The ruins look rather more 'romantic' in Hitler's painting than in photographs.

Hitler's Berlin bunker, the one in which he died, in the garden of the Reichskanzlei, was never allowed to become a ruin. It was destroyed by the advancing Russian troops, but Wolf's Lair, his headquarters on the Eastern front, still exists, and is in private ownership, getting about two hundred thousand visitors a year. Wolf's Lair was once a group of two hundred or so structures, including barracks and power stations, but chiefly comprising a series of bunkers built by the Todt Organisation, and set in six hundred acres of forest outside Kentrzyn, in Poland. Both the Germans and the Russians made attempts to destroy the complex, but it was so well built that substantial parts remain. You might think it would have become a place of pilgrimage for neo-Nazis and Hitler apologists, but in fact it seems that a lot of people were drawn there simply to shoot paintball guns and have lunch.

The pictures I've seen show it to be a bleak, crumbling, inscrutable, forbidding set of concrete blocks covered in moss

and ivy, genuinely sinister, genuinely oppressive, a formidable ruin, which in itself sent a powerful message. Still, the Polish government didn't see it that way. They recently decided that Wolf's Lair needed classing up, and insisted that the owners turn it into a place of historic and educational value. Tomasz Chincinski, one of the historians working on the project, was quoted as saying, 'At this moment, one does not feel the tragic dimension of this place.' Ah, me.

* * *

It seems that one way or another bunkers and the ruins thereof are always with us. There are still several thousand World War II pillboxes scattered around Britain, built under instructions from the Directorate of Fortifications and Works (a friendlier name than the Todt Organisation, I think) from 1940 onwards, and properly called 'hardened field emplacements'. By some accounts there were originally twenty-eight thousand of them. I always find that a walk through the English countryside is somehow cheered up by seeing a pillbox in the corner – or surprisingly often in the middle – of a farmer's field. I assume that farmers were keen to have a building they could use after the war as a store or animal pen, which indicates a certain cynicism, if also a certain optimism and confidence in the Allied Forces.

The West Coast of America is littered with bunkers, from various periods of history, designed to deter various potential invaders: Mexican, Japanese or Russian. There's a line of them all along the coast of the Presidio in San Francisco, a place for anonymous sexual encounters, I'm told; the whole area is known to some as Bad Boy Beach, though I can't say any of this was apparent when I walked there. I mostly remember seeing professional dog walkers holding the leads of groups of wildly assorted dogs.

Walk around New York City and you'll still see faded enamel signs on buildings directing you to fallout shelters. In some cases these were never much more than basement storerooms, but out in the American suburbs both public and private shelters proliferated, with much government encouragement. It seems that nobody has a figure for just how many were built, but we do know that JFK had his own presidential shelter on Peanut Island, in Florida, near the Kennedy compound in Palm Beach.

Still, this is as nothing compared to Albania, which seems to have been the bunker capital of the world, and still is in one sense, given how difficult it is to destroy a good steel-reinforced concrete bunker. Under the Enver Hoxha regime seventy-five thousand of them were built throughout the country, as protection against real or, more often, imaginary enemies. Most were simple domes, some were one-man shelters, others were big enough to have been recently converted into restaurants.

The greatest exploration, and to a large extent celebration, of the bunker comes in Paul Virilio's book *Bunker Archaeology*. Walking daily on the beach, he explored, photographed and philosophised about the concrete bunkers he saw every few kilometers alomg the French section of the Atlantic Wall, defensive structures built under Hitler's instructions from Norway to the South of France, again by the Todt Organisation. Virilio concluded that these bunkers were 'symbols of the fragility of the Nazi state. This cryptic architecture became the marker for the evolution of Hitlerian space.'

One chapter of photographs is titled 'Anthropomorphy and Zoomorphy' and I do think he's really on to something there about ruins in general, not just bunkers. Many of them do have a human or animal aspect, resembling old warlords, monarchs in exile, wounded lions, beat-up old hounds. The inclination, I think, is to see them as male, because, with exceptions, we're not much enamoured of ruined females, though this obviously doesn't apply to the Sphinx or even the Venus de Milo. One of Virilio's bunkers, actually a 'firing control tower', has the name 'Barbara' embossed in its concrete.

* * *

If you drive around the roads of Essex, in the vicinity of Brentwood, twenty-five miles or so outside London, you're likely to come upon a traffic island with a large, clear road sign directing you to the 'Secret Nuclear Bunker'. The hilarity of this wears off once you've seen it a few times, but the essential absurdity never quite does. I'm sure it's not only lovers of irony who visit the Kelvedon Hatch Secret Nuclear Bunker, although on the occasions I've been there, visitors of any sort have been extremely thin on, and below, the ground.

These days it's a privately owned tourist attraction (sorry Werner), belonging to the Parrish family who bought back the land, and with it the bunker, having been forced to sell to the government in the early 1950s. The lack of visitors is disappointing in some ways, since this is a very serious and significant bunker. It consists of three floors, the deepest more than a hundred feet below ground, tens of thousands of square feet, accommodation for six hundred people, endless rooms, a huge communications centre, government offices, a BBC radio studio, a sick bay and operating theatre, dormitories, a canteen, many long, long empty corridors to walk through; everything you'd need to shelter from a good long nuclear winter. On the other hand, the lack of visitors makes for an appropriately desolate and glum experience.

The place originally had a strictly military purpose. It was part of the ROTOR air-defence system, an elaborate radar-based scheme to detect incoming Soviet bombers – a technology that became obsolete almost as soon as it was put into service. The place then became a bunker proper and was designated a potential 'Regional Seat of Government' and then a 'Regional Government Headquarters', a difference that would always have been lost on those not privy to the convolutions of Whitehall civil-defence policy in the 1960s onwards; the bunker was in business till the early nineties. Whatever they called it, the purpose was much the same. In the event of a nuclear attack, our leaders, along with selected military and government personnel, and no doubt some of the more winsome flunkeys and lackeys, would scurry down into the bunker, stay there as long as necessary, and emerge when safe to do so to save British civilisation. The possible ways in which this project might have failed seem quite literally limitless.

The Kelvedon Hatch bunker, then, is a Cold War ruin, a place where the chosen six hundred could have survived when the South of England, and possibly the whole world, lay in ruins. I suppose you would have known in advance whether you were one of the chosen, but whether you'd have made it to the bunker, and managed to fight your way inside, is anybody's

guess. It's assumed that the Prime Minister and the Cabinet would have been in there, though whether they'd have been able to get from London to Kelvedon Hatch is another matter. The Queen however would not have been there: she was to have been flown to Canada.

To get into the bunker these days you walk across a field, along a dirt track, past signs for other better-attended attractions – the 'Rope Runners' and an ATV Course – and you find yourself in a broad, flat yard with an open-sided shed containing a broken-down military truck, and there's a slightly corroded missile on a horizontal stand and a camouflaged metal shed labelled Paint Store. Set back and raised up, presiding over the scene, is a bungalow. There's no doubt that a bungalow is what it is, and yet there's something not right about it, it's lacking some crucial essence of bungalow, and it's not quite built to human scale, it's too big and clumsy, as if it had been designed by an architect who'd had a bungalow described to him once, but had never actually seen one. In fact the building shrieks 'dodgy, covert government facility' which, as with the road sign on the roundabout, and in a more crucial way, rather spoils the bunker's claims to secrecy. Anyone looking at this place at any time in its history would have known that something furtive was going on in there.

In fact, I wonder just how secret this place ever was. The government may not have spelled out to the Parrish family exactly what they were planning to do with their field, but quite clearly they weren't building a local youth-employment centre. No doubt it was all very hush-hush, and the Official Secrets Act would have applied to all involved, but when the engineers brought in two-foot-thick blast doors, industrial air conditioners and generators, and placed a vast radio antenna on top of the hill, I'm guessing the locals might have started putting two and two together. When the powers that be shipped in large quantities of cardboard coffins, I'd have said the gig was up. The room with the cardboard coffins is, naturally, the highlight of any visit.

You enter the bunker through the bungalow, which is uninhabited, unattended, and as cheerless an interior as you could wish for. Nobody's there to welcome you, nobody offers a map or an explanation of what you're about to see. Nobody even takes your money: they do that at the end. So you're on your own. You pick up a red audio-tour 'wand', descend a set of metal stairs, and you're in a hundred-yard-long corridor, neither end quite visible despite the bare fluorescent tubes overhead. There's a ladder strapped to the wall, immensely long stretches of wiring, a few bunk beds, some Geiger counters in cases hanging from hooks. There's an ominous, or just possibly faux-ominous, sign as you start to walk along the corridor:

> It is not optional. Do NOT pass this point without a wand. So, if you do not have one, go back and get one. This really does include you.

The serious and dated authoritarian tone is set. Nobody's going to be doing any skylarking in this bunker. And frankly there's something about the feel of the place that sucks the skylarking right out of you.

And so you walk slowly through this abandoned facility, along corridors, up and down staircases, through fire doors, going from one bleak, uninhabited space to another. There are big rooms with low ceilings, small rooms with high ceilings; some of them big open-plan offices, others much more secretive and self-contained. Yes, the place has a military and industrial feel, though it also has the atmosphere of a civil-service department or tax office after hours, with a touch of the *Mary Celeste*.

There are bathrooms, of course, and narrow bunk beds with coarse wool blankets – but only two hundred of them: the sleeping was to be done in shifts. The operating theatre has a mannequin doctor, and a mannequin patient laid out on a trolley. But most of the rooms are filled with a depressing accumulation of old mismatched office furniture – retro industrial design that is still waiting to develop retro charm. Equipment seems to come from various periods in the bunker's history. There are oscillators and radios that look very World War II-boffin, but there are tables and desks crammed with computers and teleprinters that look like dreary 'state of the art' eighties' technology. It's something to do with the colour of the plastic – drab and grey and off-cream – tones that match the walls and ceilings. The overall effect is of gloom, melancholy and despair. Admittedly this isn't only an aesthetic issue: nobody expects a nuclear bunker to be a warm cheery space. There would be reasons enough for despair that have nothing to do with decor. But would it have killed them to put a bit of primary-coloured paint on the walls? Red, white or blue maybe? How about a print by John Constable? A portrait of the Queen, perhaps, to remind us of her *in absentia*?

The depression seeps into you in a number of different,

though related, ways. First there's the simple fact of being present in this place, in the here and now. The look, the feel, the blank lighting, the inertness of the air, the grubby, washed-out stillness, all combine to create a chilly, forlorn, vaguely threatening experience. I wasn't absolutely alone: there were definitely other people elsewhere in the bunker, but not many, and the place was big enough for you easily to go long periods without seeing another soul. But what if you were genuinely alone there, say you got locked in, by accident or design, say in the middle of the night? That would be utterly terrifying: and this despite the fact that you'd know you'd get out before long, and above all you'd know that the world outside was still intact. You might think there'd be some cause for optimism in all this: the bunker was never needed, the nuclear war never came, but somehow it doesn't work that way. The place reminds you of the horrors rather than banishes them.

So then you imagine that the world outside really was in ruins, that this bunker was serving its actual purpose, allowing you alone to survive when the rest of the world had been destroyed. Would anyone ever be able to tolerate that? Wouldn't you simply end it all, willingly, and join the vast community of the dead? I certainly felt that I would. But then I began to imagine something far worse, that I might be in there with five hundred and ninety-nine other people, competing for air, space, beds, status, trying to keep a stiff upper lip, trying to show *esprit de corps*, trying not to end up a snivelling wreck, as much a ruin as the world outside. I suspected I didn't have the right stuff to confront and thrive in a ruined world. This was not exactly news, and is perhaps one of the reasons I never got the call telling me I was one of the chosen six hundred.

In some of the bunker's smaller, emptier rooms, videos were being shown on chunky old TV sets, documentaries related to nuclear war and its survival. These were not offering much in the way of Werner Herzog's ecstatic truth. They included the notorious public information series *Protect and Survive*, twenty short episodes, basic animation, strangely ahead-of-its-time electronic music, and a voice-over by Patrick Allen, deeply unsympathetic and unreassuring, though you imagine he was supposed to be both.

The titles in the series included 'What to Put in Your Fallout Room' and 'Sanitation Care and Casualties'. 'Stay at Home' reminded us that fallout 'can settle anywhere, so no place in the United Kingdom is safer than any other', and my favourite single sentence comes from the episode 'Refuges': 'If you live in a caravan or other building of lightweight construction which provides you with very little protection against fallout, your local authority will be able to advise you on what to do' – and there was a cartoon image of a tiny caravan that looked like it might be blown away by a good sneeze, never mind a nuclear explosion. Actually I think that anybody who lived in a 'caravan or other building of lightweight construction' would be well aware that in the event of a nuclear attack they might not rank very high on the list of local-authority priorities. Nothing in any of the films I saw suggested that the British Prime Minister and his cronies might be lurking underground in a bunker twenty-five miles outside London.

None of this was any less scary for being so fundamentally absurd. These films, in fact everything about the bunker, this whole self-contained, post-nuclear world, was essentially risible, but also genuinely creepy, genuinely unsettling; and I suppose one of the functions of a good ruin might certainly be to put fear into the viewer and the walker, a fear both of life and death.

After I'd left the bunker and walked into the open air, via a long, cylindrical tunnel made out of corrugated metal sheeting, a little relieved but not exactly reassured, I found I was on the path that led past the bunker's sewage-treatment works. The stench hit me, would have hit anyone, like a cloud of fallout, at least that was the metaphor uppermost in my mind at the time, intense enough to make your eyes water. If that's how it smelled when the bunker was empty and not in use, how would it have smelled with six hundred people in there? Of course you could argue that when the world was in ruins there'd be nobody around to smell the miasma of sewage anyway, but that wasn't altogether consoling.

* * *

On occasions like this I find myself thinking about Speer's theory of ruin value, and I can see its appeal, but it's also kind of nuts, isn't it? Take away its mythic nationalism and it's like designing a car that's going to look great when it's rusty, or a man keeping his scalp well moisturised for the days when he's going to be bald. We know that some buildings can and do remain intact and usable for a thousand years or more, but not many, and in general we prefer it that way. Most structures have a natural lifespan, and in all but a tiny minority of cases people don't want their ruins lying around once they've outlived their usefulness. We want the remains of the old factory, the old housing estate, the old burger joint, the old nuclear shelter, got rid of, cleared away, tidied up. Let's knock it down, clear the decks and build something new in its place. Some buildings of course are ruins pretty much the moment they're built, for instance the Kelvedon Hatch secret nuclear bunker, and some are better unfinished than finished. But others – let's say the mills of Minneapolis and Stonehenge – look so much better, have so much more power ruined than in any other state.

3

The Ruins of Hollywood

> The Saint Marquis. Four o'clock. Sunset Boulevard . . . As soon as I step out of the car, I look at the pool and wonder if anybody has drowned in the pool.
>
> Bret Easton Ellis, *Less Than Zero*

> Off to my left there was an empty swimming pool, and nothing ever looks emptier than an empty swimming pool.
>
> Raymond Chandler, *The Long Goodbye*

When Edward Gibbon was on his Grand Tour of Europe in the mid-eighteenth century, he walked, like any grand tourist, in the ruins of ancient Rome. But his reaction was more intense than most. He felt himself to be treading in the footsteps of Romulus, Tully and Caesar, and experienced a profound intoxication. His diary tells us that, on 15 October 1764, as he sat in the ruins of the Capitol listening to the barefoot friars singing in the Temple of Jupiter, he conceived the idea of writing an account of the ruin of the city; in the event it took in the whole empire and became the six-volume *The History of the Decline and Fall of the Roman Empire.* And you know, I wonder if he might have felt a similar impulse if he'd been at the same party as me, in a house on the very crest of the Hollywood Hills, above Los Angeles.

It felt a lot like a movie; the house was mid-century, post and beam, with a cantilevered deck that provided one of those high, nocturnal, panoramic views that movie-makers like so much, showing the city as a taut geometrical grid of lights converging into the vanishing point. The partygoers spilled out of the house:

there were 'starlets', there were guests talking about studio deals, and there was a fairly well-known novelist braying very loudly, 'I go to these meetings with producers and they've obviously never read my work. They don't even know who I am!' Alas I did know who he was. I had even read his work, though I made sure I didn't tell him that.

To nobody's surprise, the party house had a swimming pool, actually an 'infinity pool', where the water appears to stop on the edge of space, with no deck or walkway around it. Obviously you know there's a retaining wall, that you couldn't in reality flip over the edge, be launched into space and go tumbling down the hillside, but when the pool happens to be on the very crest of the Hollywood Hills the illusion that you could is all too convincing.

A few of us walked gingerly around the three solid sides of the pool and agreed there was something terrifying about it, and we began to devise the opening of a movie. There's a girl and a guy in the pool, maybe two girls, maybe a guy and two girls, and they're naked and whooping it up, and suddenly there's a deep rumbling sound, a tremor, a quake, a harbinger of the Big One, but the kids in the pool are too loud and self-involved to hear it, and a moment later the whole hillside shifts and shudders, the walls of the infinity pool crack, then split wide open. Boys, girls, water, concrete, plumbing, all really are launched into space and really do go tumbling down the hillside which is now itself in motion. The pool, the deck, the mid-century house, the Hollywood Hills themselves, are all left in ruins.

We poolsiders liked the sound of that. And why wouldn't we? There was something very familiar about it. A swimming pool, especially a Hollywood swimming pool, communicates all kinds of messages about money, success, luxury, leisure, good times, good bodies, but we've all seen the same movies, we know it's too good to be true, and certainly too good to last. We know something bad has to happen, and there is something actually reassuring about this. Before long there'll be a corpse floating in it, à la *Sunset Boulevard*. Everybody loves *Sunset Boulevard*.

A cracked swimming pool, an abandoned pool, an empty pool, a ruined pool, that's what we're really looking for, something symbolic and emblematic. When the pool gets ruined, the people get ruined too. And sometimes we think they deserve it. We may argue about whether 'Hollywood' is the symptom or the disease, the cause or the proof of ruin, whether its citizens are in Gibbon's term 'a weak and degenerate race of beings', whether it's Babylon or Sodom or just a company town, but one way or another, a lot of people have had a lot of fun imagining it in ruins, in literature from Nathanael West in *Day of the Locust* to Steve Erickson in *Amnesiascope*, in movies from *Earthquake* to *Volcano*, via any number of others. Ed Ruscha imagined the Los Angeles County Museum of Art on fire; the artist and film designer Ron Cobb imagined Hollywood destroyed with the sign the only thing left standing. I think it's probably fair to say that the creators of these apocalyptic visions, maybe with the exception of West, have also displayed an enormous love for the city.

* * *

I had been a visitor and tourist in Los Angeles quite a few times before I came to live here in the early 2000s. One of the last of these tourist visits was at the end of 2001, very shortly after 9/11. I was living in New York at that time, and the people I met in Los Angeles had great concern and compassion for the inhabitants of New York. There was, I think, a belief that an attack on New York was an attack on the whole of the United States, and so the citizens of LA already felt involved and perhaps wounded, even though their city had not been physically harmed. At the same time there was a more specific fear that after New

York, Los Angeles was the next most obvious target for terrorists. Of course we mourned the people killed in the Twin Towers rather than the towers themselves, yet the horror had only been increased by the terrorists' choice of a landmark building, something well known to the world at large. The people of Los Angeles naturally asked themselves and each other what local landmark building the terrorists might single out as having such potent international symbolic value.

It wasn't easy to come up with an answer. As an essentially low rise, decentralised city, Los Angeles offers few conspicuous, world-renowned, easy-to-target structures. In fact there are rather more skyscrapers in LA than outsiders suppose, but few of them are famous or recognisable outside the city. LA's US Bank Tower, formerly the Library Tower, has seventy-three storeys, is a thousand and eighteen feet tall, and is indeed the tallest building in America west of Chicago, but few people know its name, and I've heard some very well-informed Angelinos refer to it as, 'You know, the one that looks like something out of *Metropolis*,' which it definitely does.

One possible target, we agreed, might be the Hollywood sign. Crashing a plane into it wouldn't have been so hard (private aircraft fly over it the whole time) and that would undoubtedly have caused panic and mayhem, but in the end it was just girders and corrugated metal in the middle of the vast, and essentially unpopulated Griffith Park. You could even argue that the Hollywood sign is in fact a ruin already, a fragment of the sign that was originally placed there to advertise the real-estate development named Hollywoodland.

Rodeo Drive in Beverly Hills was talked about. It is well known outside America as the acme of frivolous high-end luxury shopping, and might easily be regarded as a geographic centre of crass all-American materialism, but nobody could seriously imagine Islamists planning the destruction of a branch of Jimmy

Choo or Ralph Lauren as a way of delivering a blow against the Great Satan.

Other possibilities: well, the Capitol Records building is certainly a cool, conspicuous, free-standing building, but we weren't sure how wide its fame had spread. Frank Lloyd Wright's various LA buildings were definitely well-loved by some, and a vital part of the architectural heritage of the city, and a couple of them were built in high and conspicuous places, but mostly they weren't lived in, and in some cases were uninhabitable. John Portman's Bonaventure Hotel was spoken of as a possibility; the city's largest hotel, a glorious retro-futurist grouping of metallic glass cylinders, complete with atrium, glass pod elevators and a revolving restaurant. The Bonaventure was not, is not, I think, particularly well loved, but it is well known, having appeared in so many movies, from *In the Line of Fire* to *This is Spinal Tap*, and was indeed destroyed in a couple of them, including John Carpenter's *Escape from LA*.

Did terrorists turn to Hollywood movies in order to select their targets? Well, we thought that very possibly they did, and if they really had watched *Escape from LA* they'd already have seen a fairly convincing depiction of the city in ruins: the Capitol building, the LA Memorial Coliseum, and the Beverly Hills Hotel, all in rubble, Sunset Boulevard represented by a pile of rocks with a street sign stuck in it. The terrorists would have seen the glass walls of the Bonaventure popping like a Christmas-tree ornament. They'd also have seen a shoot-out in an abandoned theme park, in fact Universal City, no doubt selected because the movie was produced by Universal Studios.

And this was a consensus that grew among the citizens of LA I spoke to in that autumn of 2001: a theme park would be the perfect terrorist target. But it couldn't be any old theme park, not Six Flags or Knott's Berry Farm, not even Universal Studios. It had to be, obviously, couldn't possibly be anywhere other than, Disneyland. If you were going to spread misery and terror, if you were going to land another blow on the American heart, why wouldn't you start by ruining the 'happiest place on earth'? Admittedly Disneyland is in Anaheim rather than in the city of LA itself, but the associations are close enough; its destruction would be so symbolically weighty that it would still be regarded as an attack on LA, certainly by the kind of guys whose grasp on American realities was so flimsy that they'd thought New York's World Trade Center was actually the centre of world trade.

* * *

As a matter of fact there is an abandoned, ruined 'replica' Disneyland in China: the Wonderland Amusement Park, in Nankou Town, forty-five minutes outside of Beijing in what was formerly, and is again, a hundred-acre cornfield. This place was not destroyed by terrorists, rather it was abandoned half-finished when the money and political will ran out, when the land disputes became too troublesome for the authorities to deal with. The farmers are now back, growing crops on the empty land, and in fact the park does get plenty of visits from artists, photographers, urban explorers, fans of ruin. Would it be utterly crass to suggest that this ruined version of Disneyland might be a good deal more compelling than the thing itself?

* * *

There was a point in my life when no Saturday night was complete without one of my friends playing the Doors' album *LA Woman*. It made me learn to hate the Doors as much as love them. Sure, Jim Morrison had a way with words, but it was a hit-and-miss kind of way. Some of his lyrics were great – 'I woke up this morning got myself a beer' (considered one of the greatest lines in the Western canon by some of my Saturday-night companions); other of his lyrics were definitely not. If you wanted some lines to epitomise the pleasures and perils of

Jim Morrison's lyric-writing they were right there in the title song 'LA Woman'.

> I see your hair is burnin'
> Hills are filled with fire
> If they say I never loved you
> You know they are a liar.

The first two lines always struck me as pretty decent surrealist imagery, but then came the staggering bathos, first the rather lame rhyming of liar with fire (which was not exactly new and startling when Morrison did it in 'Light My Fire' a few years earlier) followed by simple grammatical incompetence; 'they are a liar' – come on, Jim, really.

And yet, and yet . . . now that I live in LA I realise that opening isn't surrealist imagery at all, it's more like a weather report. Some of the hills around the city really do burn every year, thousands and thousands of acres are consumed in wildfires. Some of this is perfectly 'natural' ruination and even desirable – dry trees and undergrowth, summer lightning, spontaneous combustion, a clearing out of dead wood to allow new growth: all part of the natural cycle. Some of it, inevitably, is caused by human agencies: sparks from workmen's generators, campfires that get out of control, lighted matches and cigarette butts that are tossed accidentally or deliberately. The hills around LA are an arsonist's Disneyland. In one of the first years I was here in LA, there was a major fire in Griffith Park, just a few miles up the street. Orange clouds of smoked rolled over the skyline, gorgeous, improbable and extremely scary.

Griffith Park is so vast that it doesn't conform to most people's idea of a park, certainly not an urban one. It covers about four thousand five hundred acres, and the fire that year burned over eight hundred of them. For a brief time we worried that we might lose the Hollywood sign too, and the Observatory, as well as the modern zoo up in the north-east corner. Had we lost them, we'd almost certainly have lost the ruins of the old, abandoned Griffith Park Zoo. That would have been a more minor loss admittedly, but not an insignificant one, certainly not to me.

* * *

The old Griffith Park Zoo has been listed by Weburbanist.com as a place of 'Amazing American Abandonment', which strikes me as overstating the case just a little. As sites of amazing abandonment go, it's remarkable easy to access. There's plenty of parking nearby, a children's playground, public toilets, and you'll see people having picnics and playing frisbee right outside, and sometimes even inside, the ruins. And that's one of the curious things about it: some people who use the park simply ignore the old zoo structures, and maybe they don't even see the cages and the bars and the fake rocks and cliffs, but others seem completely bewitched by them. Naturally I'm in the latter group.

The old zoo was founded in 1912, but it was rebuilt and given many of its more interesting features by the Works Progress Administration in the 1930s. No doubt everybody meant well and followed the appropriate animal-welfare regulations, and of course our attitudes to animals and their captivity have changed out of all recognition since that time, but certain of those remaining 1930s structures make it look more like a prison than a zoo: an Alcatraz for animals.

The present-day authorities address this issue by posting some slightly wheedling notices that say: 'Although these historic enclosures are no longer appropriate for housing animals, they can be home to memories of family visits . . . ' It's those words 'no longer' that seem especially uncomfortable to a modern sensibility. Surely, we think these enclosures, these constrictions, were never appropriate for housing animals.

The place closed in 1965 and a fence was put around it, but

otherwise it was left to the elements. For twenty years or so it remained as a very real ruin, a hang-out for teenagers who had no trouble scaling the fence, and occasionally it was used as a location for movies and photo shoots. When refurbishment started in the early 1980s about a dozen dangerously dilapidated structures, including the seal pond, the monkey cages and the elephant house, had to be demolished for safety reasons, and they did find an abandoned Volkswagen Beetle at the bottom of a bear pit. Nobody knows how it got there.

Today there's something thoroughly inscrutable about many of the remaining structures. You have to guess what they were, how they once looked and which animals were housed in which: was this one a monkey house or an aviary or a cage for big cats? You'd think it should be easier. What animal needed bars as thick as some of these, and were visitors really able to get as close as it now appears they could?

This is perhaps not so different from exploring any set of ruins anywhere. It's not entirely unlike going to Pompeii and trying to work out which was the Suggestum, or which was the House of the Moralist. Generally, however, when you visit classical or historic ruins, archaeologists have done some groundwork for you: there are helpful signs, some labelling, maybe a map. There's very little of that at the old Griffith Park Zoo.

The most striking and easily identifiable structures are referred to as the bear grottoes, a rather more poetic, in fact euphemistic, way of saying a bunch of pokey, gloomy, manmade, fake-looking caves. There's no sign of anything resembling a bear pit, so who knows where the Volkswagen Beetle was? The great attraction of the grottoes, however, is that you can actually go inside, climb on the fake rocks, pad along the shadowy internal passageways, press your snout against the gates and bars from the inside and gaze at the free world beyond. You can have the zoomorphic experience of feeling what it must have been like to be a caged animal here: pretty goddam awful, obviously.

A lot of people have certainly been in these places before you, and many of them seem to have come armed with spray paint. Certain parts of the grotto interiors have been turned into a kind of graffiti palace. Most of the stuff is inevitably ugly and depressing, much of it just tagging: a couple of unknown (to me anyway) taggers named Raems and Mawl seemed to have been particularly active the last time I went in there. There was even one golden oldie, though it looked pretty fresh, tagged El Barto: Matt Groening must be so proud.

Still, one or two areas were genuinely, eerily compelling, including one dark, dead-ended corridor, to which daylight didn't penetrate and which rested in deep gloom unless you had a flashlight with you, or in my case a camera with flash. I fired into the darkness, saw some painted outlines, one that looked like a camel, another like a condom with horns, and a beautifully stenciled Frankenstein head in luminous paint that swam at me out of the darkness and glowed for a couple of moments after the flash had gone. I was rather glad that even though it was fun doing this in darkness I knew there was bright sunlight outside.

You might come away from the zoo thinking, well OK, things have improved, we've made some kind of progress. We've become more compassionate, more caring about our non-human fellow creatures. Nobody today would ever dream of housing animals, or anything else, in such cramped and bleak confines as these. Well, only up to a point.

As I climbed up a set of stairs inside the back of one of the bear grottoes, I could see out through the chain-link fence stretched across the doorway at the top, and I spotted a couple of guys hanging out on the other side. I didn't think anything of it at first. I assumed they were other visitors walking in the park, which they were, though of a specialised kind.

After I came out of the grottoes I walked around the other side, to the service entrance as it were, and there were the two guys again. I could see them better now, youngish, basically healthy-looking, a Rasta and a hippie, but they weren't just visitors. They'd made a camp right there at the rear end of the grotto. They were living there in the ruins, behind the chain-link fence, invisible to passers-by, though exposed to the view of the occasional pesky, low-level urban walker who poked around in the bear grottoes. These zoo structures might not be considered 'appropriate' habitation for animals any more, but in their ruined state they were apparently quite an appealing habitat for certain human beings.

* * *

On 19 July 1936, an uncredited journalist in the *New York Herald Tribune* wrote: 'Someday, a guidebook will be written to America's most pictorial ruin – the ruins of Hollywood.' It remains unclear to me, and others, exactly what he meant. He may have been referring to old, ruined movie sets, which often remained standing on back lots after they been used, left there to weather and decay. The Babylonian set for D. W. Griffith's *Intolerance*, all bulging, fluted, stumpy columns and rearing elephants, stood in East Hollywood, more or less where Hollywood and Sunset Boulevards converge, for some years after the filming ended, from 1916 to 1919. Of course they were physically long gone by 1936, but the notion of a fake Babylon standing on Sunset Boulevard was obviously a potent symbol in the collective memory and imagination, a fascination that inspired Kenneth Anger's *Hollywood Babylon*, not published until 1959.

It is in the nature of most movie sets that they look the part without being the part. The buildings are fake, the ruins are faker. So perhaps our *Herald Tribune* scribe was thinking not of sets, but of the actual buildings of Hollywood: Grauman's Egyptian Theatre (opened in 1922) or Grauman's Chinese Theatre (opened in 1927), both built in faux-exotic styles, or perhaps he meant the Hollywood branch of the Brown Derby restaurant (opened in 1929), built in the shape of a hat. He was perhaps imagining a time when these buildings would not simply be ruined, but also inscrutable and probably meaningless, which might be also to imply that Hollywood itself was doomed, that its buildings and ideals and values were temporary, shoddy and would be swept away. Citizens of the future would need the guidebook because without it they might look at the ruins of the Egyptian Theatre and think it had been a real temple, think that the handprints in the concrete outside the Chinese Theatre might be from those who were about to be sacrificed, or that the Brown Derby was the headquarters of some kind of sinister hat cult. Incidentally the two theatres remain thoroughly in business, while the Brown Derby is long gone.

Above all, without that guidebook what will visitors of the future possibly make of the Hollywood Walk of Fame on Hollywood Boulevard and Vine Street, a series of about two and half thousand paving slabs made of marble and concrete,

each inlaid with a five-pointed star containing the symbol of a microphone, a TV, a movie camera, comedy and tragedy masks or a vinyl disc, with above it a name. I think it's fair to assume that this visitor won't recognise many, if any, of the names in the stars; some of them are unknown to all but the most dedicated film buff even now. So might the visitors think these slabs were memorials to our heroes and heroines? Our rulers? Our warriors? Our gods? Or might they think the opposite, that these were the people we held in special contempt, so much so that we walked on their very names, spat on them, let our children spill food on them, let our dogs (and occasionally our citizens) urinate all over them?

Is it even possible that they'll think these sidewalk slabs were actually gravestones; that James Brown, Myrna Loy, Fritz Lang, Matt Groening *et al.* were actually buried under the sidewalk, the way poets are buried in Westminster Abbey? Actually that misconception wouldn't last very long at all. Some of these Hollywood 'gravestones' are already in a state of considerable ruin. The ground under the slabs seems unstable, it moves and twists all the time; the slabs pop up and you can see there's no grave, no coffin or cadaver under there.

I walk along Hollywood Boulevard and Vine Street frequently, not to admire the stars, but because these streets are often on my route somewhere, and the fact is, until recently I'd pretty much stopped noticing the Walk of Fame. Occasionally I'd see somebody having their picture taken while standing on Michael Jackson, or on certain anniversaries somebody would have laid a wreath or created a small altar in memory of a certain celebrity, but I took these in my stride, just a couple more obstacles for the Hollywood pedestrian.

But when I started thinking about the ruins of Hollywood, I started looking more closely at the stars, and noticing what terrible shape some of them were in. Many, naturally, had gouges, stains and scratches, just like any other bit of pavement, and there was the occasional one with a missing letter or two. Tallulah Bankhead was looking a bit rough around the edges, but certainly she was holding up better than Ava Gardner who had a large crack across her middle, and it looked as though there had been some ham-fisted attempts at restoring her with whatever filler material was at hand.

Michael Langdon seemed to be just splitting apart, and Elliott Dexter was looking even worse, though I admit I had no idea who Elliott Dexter was till I looked him up: a silent-movie actor, star of *The Squaw Man* and *Flaming Youth*, who made his last movie in 1925. But in worst condition of all, by very much the worst, right at the southern end of the Walk of Fame, where Vine Street arrives at Sunset Boulevard, there was a star mutilated beyond recognition.

A good quarter of the paving slab, an asymmetrical chunk in the top-right-hand corner, was simply missing, filled in with a dollop of tarmac. Two of the metal star's points had therefore gone as well, and so had half of the person's name. All that was left was the first name: Franklin. Back home, some research revealed that this was the star of Franklin Pangborn (1889–1958), a successful comedy character actor in his day, dapper, bow-tie wearing, somewhere between prissy and sissy. He appeared with Dolores del Rio in *Flying Down to Rio*, and with W. C. Fields in *Never Give a Sucker an Even Break*. He also, very satisfyingly, appeared in the movie *Hollywood and Vine*, directed by Alexis Thurn-Taxis, which is about an aspiring actress whose dog becomes the star she fails to be.

I looked at this broken, ruined thing, and I thought Franklin Pangborn deserved better. In fact, I'd say just about anybody deserves better. And for a week or two I went around with this melancholy sight in my mind's eye, thinking that something should be done, though by someone else, obviously. And then I went back for another look, and I'm not sure whether things had got better or worse for Mr Pangborn. The sidewalk had been resurfaced to become a smooth black expanse, much better for walking, and Pangborn's star was no longer in ruin because it had gone completely, obliterated by tarmac. It's not hard to pick the symbolism out of that one.

Sometimes I wonder if maybe our future visitors will give us a little more credit than we deserve. Perhaps they'll see these slabs as constant reminders that life and fame are transient: sometimes the fame lasts longer than the life, sometimes vice versa. And if the stars belonging to dead, and now forgotten, personalities of the past are anything to go by, a slab of concrete and marble sometimes lasts longer than either, but, as with Franklin Pangborn, that too shall pass. Whether names are written in concrete or in water, they're erased sooner rather than later.

And perhaps our visitors will find all this extremely admirable, an indication that here was a thoughtful and philosophical civilisation, with a profound attitude towards history and transience. 'See, they placed memento mori right there in the middle of their main boulevard in Hollywood. They understood and accepted ruin and mortality, and chose to be reminded of it constantly, to celebrate the idea every time they walked down the street.'

* * *

Not long after that Hollywood Hills party with the infinity swimming pool, I went to an exhibition at the Palm Springs Art Museum, titled Backyard Oasis: The Swimming Pool in Southern California Photography 1945–1982. According to the catalogue, the swimming pool is 'a visual analogue of the ideals and expectations associated with Southern California', and the images in the show were 'an integral part of the region's identity, a microcosm of the hopes and disillusionments of America's post-World War II ethos'. OK then.

The show was large and diverse: architectural photography, still lifes with arrangements of pool chairs, cacti, garden hoses and so on, male and female pin-ups, some fashion shots, a few 'candids', some poolside movie-star portraits. The majority of the people in the photographs, it seemed to me, looked just a little too happy: they seemed to be *performing* their happiness rather than experiencing it. You could appreciate their dilemma. Hell, there they were in the sun, in California, in a pool: they damn well ought to be happy, but maybe they weren't quite as happy as they thought they ought to be. Were they contemplating death, destruction and ruination, fretting about the moment when the quake hits, the pool cracks and the water cascades down the hill? Well, I know I certainly would have been.

Inevitably I enjoyed the exhibition's photographs of empty or ruined pools much more than the intact and water-filled ones. There was a photograph by Bill Owens, for instance, showing a couple sitting at a garden table on the bottom of a waterless pool, their single-storey home visible above them at ground level. There were photographs by Craig Stecyk showing

Photograph © Loretta Ayeroff

the Dogtown Z-Boys who had appropriated, or I suppose misappropriated, empty swimming pools to use as skateboard ramps. One of my favourite empty swimming pools appeared in a photograph by Loretta Ayeroff, titled *Abandoned Pool, California Ruins, Perris Valley. 1974*. It showed a fenced, grey, empty swimming pool, drained but partly filled with rainwater. It looked solid enough and potentially usable, but it was hard to believe that anyone would ever swim in it again. Beyond the fence was a large clapboard building, industrial rather than domestic, also abandoned but not wrecked, not yet anyway, and beyond that was a stretch of scrubby semi-desert leading to distant mountains. The picture failed to give up its meaning easily. It certainly raised issues of transience and loss but not in any simple or predictable way, and it seemed to refer to a malaise far deeper and broader than concerns about the 'hopes and disillusionments of America's post-World War II ethos'.

I admit I'd never heard of Loretta Ayeroff until that exhibition, but I discovered that her Perris photograph was from a series she shot in the seventies and early eighties, under the title *California Ruins*, partly on commission for *California* magazine, and a selection of them was duly published at the time. She sounded like my kind of gal. The series included ruined sites around the whole state – Alcatraz, some military bunkers in Marin County, with the Golden Gate Bridge visible in the background, and Los Angeles' Pan Pacific Auditorium, which subsequently burned down. There were shots of abandoned gold mines, shuttered restaurants, the crumbling plaster dinosaurs in Cabazon and this particular image (see previous page) that I found, and continue to find, deeply and strangely moving.

I like the way those simple, broad concrete steps lead up to absolutely nothing, and I like that you would surely never recognise that location as California. The dull, damp sheen of the steps looks like something you might encounter in a wood in East Anglia. Those leafless shrubs and bushes are wintry in a way that's unusual in Los Angeles. The picture contains finely balanced elements of the mysterious and the banal, it's ominous yet totally deadpan.

The scene seems deliberately anonymous but the caption reads 'Huntingdon Hartford Estate', a name that means less to most people than I think it should. The estate is named for George Huntingdon Hartford (he never used that first name), who was one of those great American heirs who destroyed a fortune and himself. His family owned the A&P grocery chain. In 1922, when his father died, he was eleven years old, at which point his trust fund was worth $1.5 million a year, and when his uncle died in 1957 he inherited the rest of the estate, regularly estimated at half a billion dollars, a sum which he proceeded to lose. Mostly it went on bad business deals, but he definitely had fun along the way, as a writer and publisher, a producer of movies and plays, including his own stage adaptation of *Jane Eyre*, starring Errol Flynn.

He built a tourist resort in the Bahamas where some of *Thunderball* was shot, and he established a Gallery of Modern Art in Columbus Circle in Manhattan to show off his collection of modern art: 'It could have passed for the East Coast outpost of a private casino from the land of Mr Lucky,' according to Herbert Muschamp. These are expensive pursuits, no doubt, but it seems to have been the drugs that really made all the money disappear, and Huntingdon Hartford ended up a ruined man, a recluse – and broke, though of course these things are comparative. He actually survived in what many of us would think of as considerable comfort in Bermuda, where he lived with his daughter until 2008, dying at the age of ninety-seven.

The hundred and thirty acres of canyon that formed the Huntingdon Hartford Estate were, and indeed still are, just a couple of blocks north of Hollywood Boulevard. Huntingdon Hartford bought them from John McCormack, the Irish tenor, who had built a mansion, guest houses and a terraced garden on the property. It's not clear whether Huntingdon Hartford ever really intended to live there. He had Frank Lloyd Wright design him a Play Resort and Sports Club which, if built, would have given the impression that three flying saucers had colonised the crest of the Hollywood Hills – an appealing enough idea in its way – but a tidal wave of local opposition put an end to the plans, and although he kept the property (Errol Flynn stayed in one of the guest houses from time to time) by the end of the fifties he was ready to give the estate to the city, which promptly declined to take it.

Furious, he sold the estate at a cut price to one Jules Berman, a man who made his fortune by importing the liqueur Kahlúa into America, and who embraced ruin with a vengeance. He never intended to live on the estate there at all. He demolished the McCormack mansion and at least some of the guest houses to make way for a more orthodox housing development. No properties on the land meant no property taxes to pay, although it appears that at least one guest house was still standing at the end of the 1980s. Berman couldn't get his plans approved either, and in the end he too offered the land to the city, which this time accepted the gift, and the place is now Runyon Canyon Park.

A couple of months after I first saw Loretta Ayeroff's photographs I was having lunch with her at a coffee shop on Sunset Boulevard just down the hill from Runyon Canyon. She was grey-haired and baby faced, wore her Californian origins conspicuously and her age comfortably, more a New Ager than an old hippy, and she was happy enough to talk to me about ruin and walking. She had an interest in both.

She told me that when she was a child growing up in LA, she'd often go over to Santa Monica Boulevard where a lot of travel agents had their offices. 'I was fascinated, maybe a little obsessed, with visiting them, and acquiring free maps, posters, brochures and, if lucky, one of their travel kits filled with miniature toiletries. I'd lug these treasures home, and put them in my collection . . . I was a devoted student of Greek ruins, with a poster of the Acropolis on my wall, secretly planning my first visit there.' She's still never made it there, and has contented herself with the ruins of Los Angeles.

As well as talking about her *California Ruins*, she described another series she'd done titled *Off Wilshire*, referring to the area she was living in during the early 1980s, when her daughter was born. Every day she'd go for a walk in the neighbourhood, baby strapped to her back, camera in hand, photographing quirky, telling, undramatic details (bases of palm trees, parked cars, air vents, trash cans), observing the coming together of the quotidian, the eccentric and the enigmatic. She was, and is, interested in what Rem Koolhaas calls junk spaces, what Marc Augé might call non-spaces, the gaps, backyards, parking lots, alleyways, service streets, places that often have an element of ruin. This is a shrewd aesthetic choice, I think. There is so much about Los Angeles that is so obviously, effortlessly picturesque, and Ayeroff avoids the obvious.

We were sitting at a table outside the coffee shop and across the street there was a motel, something of a non-place in itself, a nondescript box, though it did have a very fine, swooping, retro sign that I'd photographed when I first came to live in LA and was walking the streets doing my initial 'shallow topography' of the city, beating the bounds as it were. The sign was still in good shape, and though the motel was definitely a wreck, we couldn't decide if it was actually a ruin. It was being worked on, but it was hard to tell whether it was being demolished or refurbished, perhaps a little of both. I took a photograph of Loretta with the motel in the background.

'Nice view of the ruin,' I said.

'You mean me or the motel?'

The motel, of course. The plan was that after lunch we'd go for a walk in Runyon Canyon Park to try to find those ruined steps that were in Loretta's Huntington Hartford Estate photograph. I'd been in certain areas of the park once or twice before, had certainly noticed some Beware of Rattlesnakes signs but I hadn't seen any ruins. And frankly this wasn't really my kind of territory. Sure, it was a place that offered some interesting challenges to the walker – rugged, steep, unpaved paths, bleakly hot in summer – and in return it gave you some magnificent views over Los Angeles, but the fact was, most people weren't there to walk. They were there to jog, to run, to exercise, and all too many of them were there to display themselves, to preen, the men more than the women it seemed.

We went through the gate at the south-east corner, the bottom, low end, and immediately, there they were, bang in front of us, the steps, the ones in the photograph. It had taken us all of two minutes to find them. They were so conspicuous, and so easy to find, that at first neither of us could quite believe it was the right place, and in a way we didn't want it to be. We had wanted this episode to be bigger, to involve more of a search, more of a quest.

On the other hand, although the steps were undoubtedly the right ones, and little changed (and I suppose the more low-lying and ground-hugging a structure is, the less likely it is to be ravaged by destructive forces, whether natural or human), everything around them was quite different. Those leafless, wintry trees from the photograph were not visible beyond the steps, but instead there was lush foliage and spiky blue century plants, and huge gnarled cacti grew on one side of the steps, rising well above head height, rough-looking, but in flower. You couldn't imagine all this had got there by accident. The area had evidently been landscaped, but once the plants were in place, nature had been allowed to take its rugged and unruly course. The cacti were covered with the kind of white spattering that looks like bird poop or barnacles, but is in fact the scale of cochineal worms, the kind used in red food colouring. Ridding your cactus of cochineal scale is in fact a fairly easy job, but nobody had thought that appropriate here.

We walked up the steps. What else is there to do with steps, even steps that appear to lead nowhere? And the nowhere in this case was a broad concrete slab, the base or foundation of something, a guest house we supposed (had Errol Flynn slept here?), and there were more slabs beyond, and then a dumpster, and signs of messy life – beer cans, fast-food wrappers – and rising steeply up a hillside was a set of low, straight, parallel, horizontal walls that must surely have been part of John McCormack's original terraced garden, though there wasn't much growing there now. A big, scruffy man was sitting on one of the lower levels, and he could have been homeless, living there, or he could have been another urban explorer like us. We exchanged hellos and didn't ask questions.

We pressed on but had not gone very far before I saw something in the bushes, nothing very identifiable, perhaps the end of a wall, a chunk of fallen masonry, but definitely something that looked somewhat like a ruin. I walked on, as bushes and branches spiked into my calves, while Loretta followed gamely but reluctantly, and there was yet another concrete slab, another foundation, but this one came with a substantial fireplace and a chimney made of rough stone.

My first impression was that the slab had been covered and edged in multicoloured linoleum: pieces of it appeared to have cracked and fallen on to the ground near by. But when we got close we realised we weren't looking at linoleum, we were looking at layers and layers of caked-on spray paint, maybe fifteen or twenty coats thick, graffiti sprayed on graffiti till it became three dimensional. I took a chunk of it home with me: it looks like a fragment of an unknown work by Frank Auerbach.

The chimney too had been subject to resprays from time to time, but fewer of them, since it obviously presented much more of a challenge than a flat surface: it was tall, hard to access and its surface was too rough to paint easily. On this day the base, right above the mouth of the fireplace, had some yellow and black markings, both inscrutable and graphically sophisticated, following the contours of the chimney, and above that there were abstract, geometrical patterns that made the chimney look like a hastily conceived totem pole. Less artfully someone had written BEER on the side in thin, formless capitals.

Beer had clearly been on the mind of many previous visitors. As with the terraced garden, there were cans strewn around, and more fast-food wrappers, and a couple of sleeping bags, though these didn't look like they'd been used recently. There were condoms too – unused, still in their faded yellow wrappers – the LifeStyles brand. Beer, sleeping bags, condoms: the Hollywood lifestyle indeed.

We walked on, via a ruined tennis court, up to a place called Inspiration Point to see a great, if obligatory, panorama of the city, and one that had featured in an episode of *Seinfeld*. Even here people seemed to be chiefly interested in their own physical exertions rather than their surroundings, and if they found it easy to ignore the view, they found it even easier to ignore the ruins, just as so many had at the old zoo. We hadn't seen anybody paying even the slightest attention to the ruined steps, chimney or tennis court. But as we came down the hill, we did notice a small group of half a dozen people, clustered together and looking at something very fascinating on the ground. We joined them. There, slithering rhythmically across the dry dusty path, was a five-foot-long snake. Someone said, 'It's a rattler,' but it quite obviously wasn't: it had no rattle. And eventually a consensus was reached that it was a very fine, very big rat snake, not the tamest or least snappy of creatures, but nothing that would kill you.

What is a canyon, Loretta and I said afterwards, without a snake, a garden without a serpent, an estate without a ruin? On the other hand, we did agree that our walk might have been even better if Frank Lloyd Wright's flying saucers had been looming over us on the horizon.

* * *

If you want to live in a ruin, find a house, move in, and wait a while. If you buy a house built by Frank Lloyd Wright, you may not have to wait any time at all. The moment anyone hears the name Frank Lloyd Wright they also hear the rumours, or perhaps urban myths, or perhaps hard facts, about the imperfections in his buildings, above all the leaking roofs.

One of the most famous stories concerns Wingspread, a house in Wing Point, Wisconsin, commissioned from Wright in the late 1930s by Herbert 'Hib' Johnson, of Johnson Wax. Shortly after the project was completed, Wright, who was then enjoying the dry desert heat of Arizona, received a phone call from Johnson. It was a rainy night in Wing Point, and Johnson was in his house, entertaining and no doubt trying to impress some guests, and he was calling to inform Wright that water was coming through the ceiling. He said something like, 'Frank, you built this beautiful house for me and we enjoy it very much. But I've told you the roof leaks, and right now I'm with some friends and distinguished guests and it's leaking right on top of my head!'

'Well, Hib,' said Wright, 'why don't you move your chair?'

Hilarity ensued.

Well, a leaking roof is not in itself synonymous with ruin, though it may well be the start of the process. Certainly it rains much less in Los Angeles than in a lot of places where Wright built houses. LA has averaged about thirteen inches of annual rainfall over the last thirty years. However, the first winter I lived here, 2004/5, we had 37.96 inches: there really hadn't been anything like it since the nineteenth century. The roof of our house leaked, and so did the roof of everybody else I talked to in LA. Frank Lloyd Wright's buildings, of course, did not escape. And it was in the middle of that rainy season that I first walked inside Wright's Ennis House, in Hollywood.

The Ennis House (it was known as the Ennis Brown House for part of its history) is set high on a hill close by Griffith Park, a massive, solid, fortress-like thing, looking both futuristic and ancient, like a space-age Mayan temple, or perhaps like space-age Mayan ruins. It's appeared in all kinds of movies, from *Bladerunner* to *The House on Haunted Hill*, and in endless photo-shoots, including a famous one by Helmut Newton showing a statuesque, bare-breasted model walking across the courtyard to her car. The camera is generally able to find an angle that makes the Ennis House look solid and in good condition, but of course the camera deceives.

I did my tour of the house on a morning after a rainy night. Parts of the outside of the house were draped in tarpaulins, and inside there were plastic sheets and buckets all over the place. Even so, these hadn't caught all the water; some of the floors were wet, some of the ceilings sagged, certain walls were sodden top to bottom. This was right in the middle of a multi-million-dollar renovation.

In fact there had been problems with the house's structure right from the beginning: construction started in 1924. Wright fell out with his client early on (he did a lot of that) and his son Lloyd Wright took over. The house utilised Wright's 'textile block' system, concrete slabs moulded on site using the granite from the ground on the site. Some of these blocks crumbled even as the house was being built, and some of them are still crumbling today.

There was, and still is, a massive retaining wall on the southern side of the property, giving the house the giant-fortress look, and at the time I made that first visit a lot of the textile blocks had fallen away, leaving great cavities behind, and fragments of the blocks had slid down to the bottom of the hill, right to the chain-link fence. Without much difficulty anyone could reach in, grab a chunk of the fallen concrete, and become the owner of a small piece of a Frank Lloyd Wright building. Mine sits in a small display case next to my desk, right beside my model of Stonehenge.

I go over to the Ennis House from time to time, it's walking distance from where I live, and I stroll around the outside of the building (public access is only on a few special days a year), and it does look as though progress has been made recently. It looks much less of a ruin. There are still some crumbling concrete textile blocks but not so many that you can reach in and take a sample. And on the north-east corner there's a gorgeous, broken column, swathed in ivy, but its ruined state allows you to see exactly how the textile-block system works. It looks as picturesque as any ruin in the classical world, if rather less likely to make it through the centuries.

In fact, that rainy winter of 2004/5 was not the worst thing to have happened to the Ennis House. About a decade earlier it had been a victim of the Northridge Earthquake. This was not quite the Big One that Angelinos anticipated, and still do, but it was big enough. It struck early on 17 January 1994, at 4.31 in the morning, and lasted about twenty seconds. It was a 6.7 magnitude quake, which is not devastatingly high, but the ground speed was one of the highest ever recorded in an American urban area. People felt the earth move in Las Vegas, two hundred and seventy miles away. In LA itself buildings fell apart, freeways collapsed, nearly nine thousand people were injured, $20 billion of damage was done, and fifty-seven people were killed. That's by no means a trivial number, but it does seem surprisingly low, given the severity of the quake.

There were some ironies attaching to the event, naturally. Universal Studios decided, out of respect, to shut down its Earthquake ride, based on the 1974 movie. And Disneyland did close briefly, though only for a safety inspection, not because there was any damage. Everything at the happiest place on earth was found to be intact, no sign of ruin whatsoever.

I was living in England then and I followed the story as well as I could from that distance, but it was only later that year when I actually stood outside one of Frank Lloyd Wright's other projects, Hollyhock House, in Barnsdall Park, down on Hollywood Boulevard, very close to where Griffith's *Intolerance* set once stood, that the enormity of the event struck me. I immediately saw ominous vertical cracks running through the concrete walls of the main building, from foundation to roof. Concrete lumps lay around on the ground outside, lumps far too big to pick up and carry home, and in any case I was being closely supervised by a guide. The gardens were scorched, not a hollyhock in sight.

Hollyhocks were the favourite flower of Aline Barnsdall, the oil heiress who commissioned Wright to build what she envisaged as a high-minded artists' colony, which would have had studios, a theatre, living accommodation and a small zoo. You can imagine how well that worked out: Hollyhock House is now owned by the city. It's another example of 'Mayan revival' – only a mile and a half from the Ennis House, both on hillsides, each providing a great view of the other.

Hollyhock was only Wright's second project in California, and he wasn't able to supervise the construction directly because he was designing the Imperial Hotel in Tokyo. This was the building that survived several earthquakes, thanks to its floating foundations and flexible walls. During the Great Kanto Earthquake of 1923, which struck on the day the hotel was due to open, the Imperial was used as a shelter for survivors. A hundred and fifty thousand people died in that one, but Wright obviously didn't think floating foundations and flexible walls were necessary in sunny California, although actually I think that the site simply didn't allow for them.

Things looked pretty desperate that first time I visited the Hollyhock. The damage looked structural rather than superficial, but if the guide was to be believed things weren't in fact as bad as they looked, there was an up side to the earthquake. The house had been fortunate enough to have insurance. Since 'Northridge', as Angelinos always refer to it, earthquake insurance has become a luxury that few in the city can afford, but back then the insurance companies still thought it would never happen, and so had provided cover for the Hollyhock. The insurance money, said the guy showing me round, would not only pay for the earthquake repairs, it would pay for work that had needed doing even before the earthquake. I'd have thought insurance companies were wise to that kind of thing but perhaps they considered it good public relations.

That first visit was nearly twenty years ago, and I've been going back ever since. When people come to town I often take them on a Frank Lloyd Wright walking tour, from one 'ruin' to another. We stroll around the grounds of Barnsdall Park, where things sometimes look pretty good – there are now hollyhocks growing in quantity there – and then we take a tour of the house, where things are generally looking less good. When I last did it, the place still looked like a wreck, there were wall-size sheets of plastic hanging vertically, and the cracked concrete revealed the rebar underneath, which again was very interesting if you wanted an insight into the house's construction, but less appealing if you just wanted to see beautiful architecture. The last time I tried to take somebody there, just a few weeks ago, the place was again closed for renovation.

Now, of course, you could say that any house needs constant attention, and the greater the house the greater the need. But what's going on at Hollyhock House never looks like simple maintenance, it looks as though the house is the scene of an epic, elemental struggle between order and chaos, between construction and destruction. Vast amounts of money and energy are constantly being spent in an attempt to stop the house sliding into complete and utter, and perhaps ultimately inevitable, ruin.

* * *

When I moved to Los Angeles one of my first, not-very-well-thought-out plans was to walk every street in Hollywood, in a systematic, regimented way. Many of the streets are laid out on a grid pattern, and that appealed to the minimalist-slash-conceptualist in me. But problems presented themselves immediately. For one thing, the exact boundaries of Hollywood are a matter of some debate: the tour guides, the cops, the one-time secessionists, the real-estate agents, all have competing beliefs about where Hollywood begins and ends. One broadly accepted notion, however, is that Mulholland Drive is the northernmost boundary, and that's a problem in itself. I've walked certain sections of Mulholland, but only a man with a death wish would seriously want to walk its length and have to deal with its blind bends and non-existent sidewalks as it curls all the way along the top of the Hollywood Hills.

Another problem was the Hollywood Freeway, the 101. Since it slashes diagonally across the grid of streets, corner to corner, north-west to south-east, the Hollywood walker encounters it all over the place. You're always having to go under it or over it, and in the beginning both options struck me as equally daunting. There were a couple of bridges crossing it that had incredibly low railings, just about waist high, and you could easily have leaned over them, heard the roaring siren song of the cars below and been drawn to certain earthbound and unheroic doom.

Walking under the freeway was no picnic either. There are underpasses, but these are again Rem Koolhaas's junk spaces. You know that somebody must have *designed*, or at least engineered, them, but essentially they seem to be off-cuts of architecture and place, the bits and pieces that happen to be left over when more urgent structural concerns have been met. And even though there are sidewalks in these underpasses, these are conduits made for automobile traffic, and it doesn't seem that anybody has ever considered what it might feel like to walk along them: never comfortable, and sometimes downright scary. Not that traffic is the sole problem. I know of just one pedestrian-only freeway underpass, connecting two sections of North Kingsley Drive, between Santa Monica Boulevard and Melrose Avenue. It's about as pedestrian-friendly as a snake pit: narrow, low-ceilinged, walls thick with graffiti-proof paint and floor-to-ceiling graffiti. There's light at the end of the tunnel but you know you wouldn't get halfway there before the pursuing zombies had ripped your legs off.

Initially, I didn't engage with the freeway while walking. The areas around it became blank spaces on my mental map of the city, and equally blank parts of my walking experience. But after a while I realised that simply wouldn't do. I was enough of an urban explorer and a contrarian, to think that engaging the very thing you don't want to engage with was what my LA walking experience might ultimately be all about. This also coincided with a growth spurt in my ruinophilia. I decided to embrace the freeway, which is to say I decided to embrace walking in the ruined spaces around it.

These places are by no means *abandoned* ruins. An intense life of one kind or another thrives around the freeway: there are houses and apartment blocks, even motels, that snuggle up to the 101 and have balconies with panoramic views of the traffic jams, and direct access to clouds of hydrocarbons. Meanwhile, down at ground level, freeway on and off ramps are places to do business: some guys are selling bags of oranges, others are chilling out, playing guitar, holding up cardboard signs saying they just want to get a little money for a motel room for the night. There's also vigorous plant life: vines that creep up the concrete pillars and parapets and are threatening to make the freeway look like a jungle ruin, even while it's still in use.

The intersection of straight streets and diagonal freeway creates strange little pockets of unused land, many of them roughly triangular in shape. Some look quite hospitable, some look desolate. Some are closed off by high fences and locked gates, while others are completely accessible, enabling you simply to walk on to the freeway if that's what you want to do. On Van Ness Avenue somebody has adopted a patch of ground between the off ramp and the parking lot of Tommy's burger joint, then turned it into a flowerbed complete with euphorbia and variegated agaves.

Other, larger areas are put to less decorative uses. There's a large thin slice of downward sloping land on the south side of Sunset Boulevard, next to a Saab garage, that anybody can walk into, and obviously many have, me included. In the daytime you'll usually find nobody home, but there's always plenty of evidence of habitation: blankets, old clothes, the occasional mattress, even pages torn from a Bible, tarot cards, the odd battered teddy bear. It's as though the props department has been busy, if not especially inventive. These are the homes of the homeless, improvised temporary constructions, sometimes oddly inventive and surprisingly homey. There was, very briefly, a guy who lived under the freeway at the corner of Franklin Avenue and Argyle Street who had a pile of twigs and branches that he'd made into a chicken coop, complete with a single chicken.

There is one freeway underpass that I actually like walking through, that I've even taken people to as part of an 'alternative Hollywood' walk. It's the North Cahuenga Boulevard underpass, a place that provides a unique experience of freeway-adjacent space. If you drive through it the experience is nothing at all, but on foot it's definitely something. The bridge supporting the freeway is broad and gently curved and when you stand under it you see that overhead the freeway is divided into separate northbound and southbound lanes, with a gap between them, and filling that gap is a long, narrow skylight made of glass tile. This isn't in the usual sense 'stained glass' though there's certainly plenty of staining: inky blues and earth browns caused by who knows what – oil, carbon, decomposing vegetation, road gunk, maybe roadkill? Even so, the light that filters down is eerily appealing. It's not exactly like being in a cathedral, there's nothing very spiritual about it, but you're definitely standing in a strange, compelling, uplifting architectural space. People on foot just don't belong there, which is a large part of the attraction, the very best reason to be there. I can stand for long periods of time looking up at the light, hearing the rubber and concrete roar of the traffic overhead, basking in the weird, brutal, accidental elegance of it.

And while I'm there I indulge in some of the typical Angelino thoughts of apocalypse. What if I was walking here right when the Big One hit? I imagine the fragmented glass, the pulverised concrete, the spears of rebar, the falling cars coming down from on high, and there I'd be below, defenceless, out of place, a pedestrian in the ruins, who wouldn't stand even half a chance.

* * *

Need I say that I do not have earthquake insurance on my own house. I don't have an earthquake preparedness kit either; and although I assume there must be plenty of people in LA who do, asking around, I've only found one person in my circle who does: he keeps one in his house, another in his car. Are the rest of us short-sighted? Yes, I suppose we are. Do we think it will never happen? No, no, most of us are pretty confident that it will happen sooner or later, it's just a question of how *much* later. We could all have moved on or be dead by then, if we're lucky.

On the other hand I'm usually able to convince myself that the house is reasonably secure. The structural engineer Arthur Levin, famous for working on houses that cling to the Hollywood Hills, consulted on the foundation. Levin is still alive and active at the time of writing, aged ninety-four, and is the author of *Hillside Building*, a manual for those who want to build houses in ludicrous places. The book, according to its blurb, contains examples 'of the author's triumphs and occasional enlightening failures'. Well OK, so there's no reason to feel totally smug; let's just hope that my house will not be the source of his further enlightenment.

Actually there is evidence to support our feelings of (comparative) security. The people we bought the house from were living here at the time of the Northridge Earthquake. While Hollyhock House and the Ennis House, both of them less than a couple of miles away, were splitting open like coconuts, while one of my friends was woken by a collapsed ceiling and a brand-new view of her neighbour's apartment through one bedroom wall, and a view of Sunset Boulevard through the other, our house's previous inhabitants remained blissfully asleep in their bed, untroubled and unaware.

Personally I have never felt so much as a tremor in LA, neither in the house or elsewhere, even when people around me have. There was an afternoon as I was walking to meet somebody for lunch and a postman came bounding along the street towards me, wide-eyed, grinning, quite giddy with excitement. 'Did you feel it?' he said. 'Did you feel it?' He'd been driving his mail van and the shock had thrown the vehicle across the road. Surely, he said, since I was on foot, I must have felt it even more intensely? I don't think he altogether believed me when I said I hadn't felt a thing. But why would you lie about something like that?

I'm sure his giddiness would have evaporated pretty rapidly in the event of real disaster. He wasn't taking pleasure in the prospect of Los Angeles being reduced to rubble, he was experiencing relief that it hadn't been. Even so, to know that ruination might be so close in some ways puts you on your mettle, makes you feel more alive. And maybe it's also a way of compensating for having a good life, good weather and in some cases (though not my own) a swimming pool. Yes, we say, it's true that we have these good things going for us, but it could all be in ruins in the blink of an eye. You're so much better off living in Slough or Woking. Honest. Or even Sheffield.

4

The Ruins of Sheffield

> Sheffield's form, as a northern industrial city, has been mythologised through function. The footprint of heavy industry has remained despite the encroachment of economic rationalisation, which left behind its steel mills and factories as empty husks, a reminder of an earlier model of globalisation and industrial hegemony. However, as a city it has redefined itself aurally, characterised through a bricolage of archaic industry and shiny technology, the city's rhythms have reverberated through popular music forms.
>
> Stephen Mallinder, 'Sheffield is not Sexy'

John Ruskin, 1819–1900, author of *The Seven Lamps of Architecture* and *Modern Painters*, was fond of ruins, walking and Sheffield, just like me, though there the resemblance ends. In Volume IV of *Modern Painters*, in a chapter titled 'Of the Turnerian Picturesque', he examines the extent to which J. M. W. Turner 'has admitted into his work the modern feeling of the picturesque, which, so far as it consists in a delight in ruin, is perhaps the most suspicious and questionable of all the characters distinctively belonging to our temper, and art'. It significant that he sees an interest in ruins as modern: we might have thought it was ancient, or eternal.

Ruskin is understandably suspicious of a 'delight in ruin', but equally, since in his estimation Turner is essentially beyond reproach, and since Turner delights in ruin, Ruskin posits the notion of two kinds of picturesque, the higher and the lower. In Ruskin's reckoning the artist (and surely the non-artist too) who enjoys the lower picturesque is essentially heartless. 'All other men feel some regret at the sight of disorder and ruin. He alone delights in both; it matters not of what. Fallen cottage – desolate villa – deserted village – blasted heath – mouldering castle – to him . . . all are sights equally joyful.' The higher picturesque, however, 'depends upon largeness of sympathy', which Turner, says Ruskin, has in spades. Turner doesn't simply appreciate the form and the look of a ruin, he is profoundly moved by the broader *meaning* of that ruin.

Well, this is persuasive and potentially flattering. Which of us wouldn't prefer to think of ourselves as connoisseurs of the higher picturesque? Who wouldn't want to have a largeness of sympathy? We're not just rubber-necking rubes, we're people with heart and sensitivity. We want to feel and understand those deeper meanings. On the other hand, how many ruin lovers, myself included, can put hand on heart and claim that we absolutely always live up to our own highest ideals. How many of us have looked at a collapsed house or an abandoned factory and thought, 'Man, that looks cool!' long before we've given any thought to the people whose lives may have been ruined by that collapse or abandonment?

Ruskin himself, I think, sometimes talked a better game than he played. He had, from childhood, a great affection for architectural ruins. He writes in *Praetorita*: 'all architecture . . . depended with me for its delight on being partly in decay. I revered the sentiment of its age, and I was accustomed to look for the signs of age in the mouldering of its traceries, and in the interstices deepening between the stones of its masonry.' I'm not sure there's a great deal of higher sympathy there. He's enjoying decay and signs of age for their own sake, isn't he? He did, however, also write, in *The Seven Lamps of Architecture*: 'When we build, let us think that we build for ever . . . ' which might provide examples of mouldering traceries and deepening interstices, though by definition it would never provide any actual ruins. It would be great fun if, via some warp in the space/time continuum, we could see Ruskin arguing with Albert Speer about this, and about ruin theory.

On other occasions, when Ruskin was walking in ruins, he more successfully lived up to his own higher ideals. One of his diary entries, which appears as a footnote in that Turner essay, recounts a walk in Amiens. He writes:

> Amiens, 11th May, 18—. I had a happy walk here this afternoon, down among the branching currents of the Somme; it divides into five or six – shallow, green, and not over-wholesome; some quite narrow and foul, running beneath clusters of fearful houses, reeling masses of rotten timber . . . Miserable little back yards, opening to the water . . . an old flamboyant Gothic church, whose richly traceried buttresses sloped into the filthy stream; all exquisitely picturesque, and no less miserable. We delight in seeing the figures in these boats pushing them about the bits of blue water, in Prout's drawings; but as I looked today at the unhealthy face and melancholy mien of the man in the boat pushing his load of peats along the ditch, and of the people, men as well as women, who sat spinning gloomily at the cottage doors, I could not help feeling how many suffering persons must pay for my picturesque subject and happy walk.

He stops himself saying the Victorian equivalent of 'Man, that looks cool!'; he's not simply getting off on the rot and the filth, although naturally this stuff is much easier to pull off in print.

Ruskin also wrote, 'Walk while ye have the light, lest darkness come upon you.' He walked extensively in the Alps, the Lake District and in London, and in the Peak District, and even in Sheffield. Ruskin's fondness for Sheffield didn't induce him actually to live in the place, but he visited often enough, set up a commune there for idealistic socialists, and the Guild of St George, which he founded, assembled a collection of paintings (including one watercolour by Turner), books, manuscripts, coins and geological specimens which were first displayed in a museum in Walkley, which was, and still is, a rough-edged but striving part of the city. The current Ruskin Gallery is part of the Millennium Galleries in Sheffield's 'Cultural Industries Quarter'.

Ruskin created his Guild of St George collection for the education and edification of local working men, and he much admired the skilled metalworkers of Sheffield, even as he disapproved of most technological and industrial developments. He especially disapproved of the railways since in his opinion they ruined the landscape and in many cases necessitated the demolition and ruination of perfectly serviceable buildings. His most famous diatribe against the railways refers to Monsal Dale, to the building of what is known locally as the Monsal Dale Viaduct, more correctly the Headstone Viaduct, in Derbyshire, just a little way south of Sheffield. He wrote: 'That valley where you might expect to catch sight of Pan, Apollo and the Muses, is now devastated. Now every fool in Buxton can be in Bakewell in half an hour, and every fool in Bakewell at Buxton.'

The quotation is from one of a series of letters addressed to 'the Workmen and Labourers of Great Britain' that appeared as pamphlets in the 1870s and were collectively published as *Fors Clavigera*, a title, I suggest, that might not have had workmen and labourers immediately rushing to their local pamphlet seller. In fact, Ruskin's views on the ruination of landscape are more complicated than this might suggest. He suspected that the earth itself had already started to slide into ruin, and was no longer the perfected place it had been. In the fourth volume of *Modern Painters* he notices that some parts of the Alps are considerably less beautiful than others, and asks, 'Is this, therefore, the earth's prime into which we are born: or is it, with all its beauty, only the wreck of Paradise?'

Growing up in Sheffield, I never heard anybody mention the name John Ruskin, and there was no Ruskin Museum in the city at that time, but I did know Monsal Dale as a place the family sometimes went on a Sunday afternoon. I don't think we ever did much of anything there except walk about, which I suppose was the whole point. I have half-convinced myself that I can remember being down at the bottom of the dale, on the banks of the River Wye, and looking up to see trains pass over the viaduct and disappear into a tunnel in the hillside, but I may be falsifying the memory.

Recently, on a Sunday afternoon at the end of the summer, I went there again with my oldest friend and sometime walking companion Steve, who is Sheffield born and bred, and still resident. I had told him I was writing a book about walking and ruin, and he was enthusiastic about the idea. There were reasons why it resonated with him. Steve looks a fit enough man, and is on some days, but he's regularly brought down by back pain that incapacitates him for a week or two at a time, and when that drifts away, he sometimes gets sciatica which causes hot stabs of pain that shoot down the sciatic nerve in the back of his leg. I'm sympathetic and I count my blessings. I'd have understood if he'd bailed on the Monsal Dale expedition but he was perfectly game.

Other kinds of physical ruin were much on his mind too. His mother, in her eighties, was diagnosed as having the early stages of Lewy Body Dementia, one of the universe's more sinister bad jokes, a condition that resembles Parkinson's or Alzheimer's in some ways, but has more ornately horrific symptoms that include hallucinations, insomnia, the acting out of dreams, the inability to stand or walk, or swallow or excrete. Steve said he felt that his mother was falling into decay, slipping away, becoming a husk, a ruin. A walk in Monsal Dale might just possibly, very briefly, take his mind off things.

We started at the car park outside the Monsal Head Hotel. There was an ice-cream van, and a lot of leather-clad motor-bikers, though of a very chic and stylish kind, and they would not, it seemed, be doing any walking. You could understand why some people might be content with a merely visual experience. Even from the car park you have a spectacular view of Monsal Dale, a deep, clean fold in the landscape, rugged but softened by lush greenery, rolling hills and dense clumps of trees, dramatic but not forbidding. And the Headstone Viaduct runs across the valley, about halfway between river and peak, a sharp straight horizontal linking the two sides of the dale, tying them, and the view, together. The viaduct has five regular, honest, no-nonsense arches, stone and brick, various shades of sandy brown, all the same density of colour as the greenery around it. Despite what Ruskin says, it fits in beautifully. At this point in history it's hard to see the viaduct, this solid and substantial piece of nicely weathered Victoriana, as anything other than 'picturesque' in the most ordinary sense of the word. It looks good. It doesn't look out of place. It doesn't seem to ruin anything.

Ruskin might be somewhat cheered by the current state of things in Monsal Dale. The railway has gone, and although the viaduct remains, no trains run across it, and haven't since 1968. On first sight, from a distance, it didn't, strictly speaking, seem to be all that much of a ruin, but it was certainly a remnant, a fragment of a defunct and no longer viable system, a reminder, a relic. The fools in Buxton and Bakewell now go back and forth by car, and the viaduct is the preserve of walkers, cyclists and the very occasional horse rider. From our place at the edge of the car park we looked down and saw a couple of pedestrians crossing it. We determined to join them.

This was harder than anticipated. We took what seemed to

be the obvious path, the one that looked as though it would lead us directly down to the viaduct, but before long it was clear that we were heading in quite the wrong direction. The viaduct was now behind us, and we were walking away from it, alongside an increasingly broad stretch of water with no crossing place. Reluctant to turn back, reluctant to admit our mistake, we kept going till we met another walker, a large, jolly young woman, and we asked her if we could get to the viaduct this way. She assured us we could, so we went on. After a while we wished we'd pressed her to explain exactly how we could get to the viaduct this way, since we very definitely weren't getting any closer, and a little after that we began to wonder if perhaps the woman didn't actually know what a viaduct was, especially when we came to a weir, which made the river broader still. Maybe the woman had thought 'viaduct' was another name for weir.

Fortunately Steve knew his history and wasn't afraid to repeat it. He recalled the Duke of Wellington at the Battle of Assaye, a reference that was lost on me at the time. The battle, he explained, took place in the Second Maratha War, in central India, in 1803. Wellington, who was still Arthur Wellesley at the time, was leading British and East India Company forces against two Maratha chiefs. Unexpectedly, and after he'd split his force, Wellington spotted the Marathas across the other side of the Kaitna River, at the village of Assaye. Outnumbered and outgunned, he nevertheless decided to attack. There was a ford at that point in the river, and although it would have been possible to cross right there, it would also have been suicidal. His guides assured him there was no other crossing place, but Wellington didn't believe them. He deduced, noting the locations of other nearby villages, that there must be another crossing somewhere else, so he sent his men to reconnoitre, and sure enough one of them found another ford not so far away, and Wellington took his troops across and launched a surprise attack; thoroughly bloody, but militarily successful. We, Steve suggested, should do something similar.

Like Wellington, he deduced that there must be a crossing somewhere near by. I hoped it wasn't a ford that we'd have to wade through, and preferably not some treacherous stepping stones, and sure enough it was neither of these. Just a few minutes later it was proved that Steve's deduction had been correct when we came to a small, solid, perfectly serviceable, perfectly ordinary footbridge. Once across we'd be able walk back along the other side of the river, and assuming there were no warring Marathas in the way, we'd come to the viaduct.

And that's what we did. We'd come a very long way round, but we told ourselves that the journey was the destination, and at last we were at the viaduct: unfortunately at ground level, down at its foot. The arches swooped grandly fifty feet or so above our heads, and from this angle the viaduct looked more picturesque and nobly proportioned than ever, and also a little more ruined. Creepers and moss were running wild in places, and we could see up into the arches where some of the stones looked loose. There was also a sign on the arch that read 'Rope Swinging and Abseiling Prohibited', and some steel wires were in place beneath the arches to prevent the swinging if not the abseiling. We hadn't suspected this was such a wild, lawless or athletic place.

In any case, we were still at the base of the viaduct, and the whole point of the exercise had been to walk *along* the viaduct, not under it. It required a steep ascent and a bit of scrambling up a hillside before we got to the top and set foot in the place where the rails had once been. As we walked across, Steve told me this was the site of the worst and, he insisted, the only, dirty trick he ever played on his two sons.

Some years back, when the boys were aged six and eight, he'd brought them to walk across the viaduct, much as we were doing now, though the place had been slightly different then. The tracks were already gone, but at that time the mouth of the Headstone Tunnel, which we were walking towards, at the far end of the viaduct, had been boarded up with a couple of solid wooden doors, creating a dead end. Steve went ahead of his boys, walked up to the doors and peered through a crack into the darkness of the empty tunnel. Then he feigned exaggerated panic, turned urgently to his kids and yelled something like, 'Oh no, there's a train coming. Run for it!' and began to bolt frantically back across the viaduct, the way they'd come.

Gullible and obedient, the kids panicked for real, were absolutely terrified, and ran desperately in the same direction as their dad, until at some point Steve stopped running and turned around, laughing just a little guiltily. He hadn't really meant to scare his boys so much. He'd thought they were old enough and wise enough to have noticed that since there were no tracks running along the viaduct there would be no trains either, but the kids were in reality still very young and naïve, and above all they'd made the mistake of trusting their dad. Steve, a man with pedagogic instincts (consider his educating me about the Duke of Wellington), decided to make this a teachable moment, and pointed out to his lads that even if there *had* been trains and tracks it would certainly have made no sense to try to outrun the train. The sensible thing would have been to clamber up the embankment at one or other side of the tunnel mouth; although, looking at it now, he reckoned there wasn't much embankment in evidence. Perhaps hurling themselves off the viaduct into the river would have been the better course.

Now the tunnel mouth was open, the wooden doors were gone, and you could walk right inside. Poking around in abandoned railway tunnels is pretty much heaven for the lover of ruin, for 'infiltrators' of any stripe, though this one was extremely well ordered. There were numerous health and safety notices: not to enter when the lights were off, to be on the look out for horses, to keep to the left, not to touch the tunnel walls. We walked on the right, and of course I felt obliged to touch the walls even though I might otherwise have had no urge to. And after we'd gone a little way inside, we saw that the tunnel had a sharp bend to it, and I suspected you wouldn't have seen a train coming until it was far too late.

But fortunately the light at the end of the tunnel is sometimes just daylight, and in due course we emerged at the other end. We stepped out of the tunnel mouth into a tightly constricted space, a railway cutting, a deep gouge in the earth, and what looked like some honest-to-goodness ruin. Rising up both sides of the cutting were brick pillars, or piers, of various ages and styles, some much cruder and older than others, some of them appearing ancient or even classical. They looked liked columns that might once have supported a floor or a roof, and certainly they looked rough and irregular in places. But the more we looked the more it seemed they weren't the remains of any larger structure, of any ruined civilisation, but had been built solely to keep the walls of the cutting from falling on to the train tracks, and now on to walkers, cyclists or the occasional horse rider. They had the attractive look of ruin even as they remained functional.

Would John Ruskin have been satisfied with a walk like this? Here in the broadest sense was ruin. Here was the confirmation that his despised railways were gone and here were some rough but surprisingly elegant remains to prove it. There was a certain amount of decay, there were signs of age, mouldering traceries, interstices deepening between the stones of the masonry. The place was picturesque, and not in the lower sense. Surely Ruskin would have had to love a walk across the Headstone Viaduct and into the tunnel and its cutting, wouldn't he? It might not have had the same splendour as walking in the Alps or among the stones of Venice, but it was surely as good as walking through Amiens. I like to think he'd have thought so, anyway. I wonder how he'd have felt about Jarvis Cocker and Pulp.

* * *

'Intake, Manor Park, The Wicker, Norton, Frecheville, Hackenthorpe, Shalesmoor, Wombwell, Catcliffe, Brincliffe, Attercliffe, Ecclesall, Woodhouse, Wybourn, Pitsmoor, Badger, Wincobank, Crookes, Walkley, Broomhill, Oh!' These are the opening words to the Pulp song 'Sheffield Sex City', and are spoken by Jarvis Cocker, over some slow, jazzy, organ noodling.

I'm not sure just how strange these words sound to non-Sheffielders – they're all the names of places in and around the city – but to locals or (as in my case) former-locals, they're extremely familiar. My dad was born in Attercliffe. I went to school in Broomhill, and of course photographed ruin there. I had friends in Crookes, a girlfriend in Norton, an aunt and uncle in Manor Park, or 'on the Manor' as we always said. I used to walk through some of these places all the time. Nevertheless, hearing them in this musical, spoken-word context makes the familiar sound downright peculiar. Wombwell? Frecheville? Badger? How did they even come up with these names? Well, of course, there are perfectly good historical explanations for some of them – Wombwell is derived from 'well in a hollow' in Old English, Frecheville was the name of a local family, but that still doesn't make them sound any less strange, and I still haven't found a derivation for Badger.

When Sheffield was in its full industrial, steel-making glory, say from 1830 to 1970, it was widely regarded as a kind of hell. A photograph of the Hadfield Steelworks, taken by E. O. Hoppe in 1925, shows the city apparently submerged in clouds of sulphur. The air, the landscape, the buildings, the people, were filthy with industrial pollution: bad health was a given. To walk past a steelworks, something I did once a week every time I went to visit my grandparents, was to catch a glimpse of a violent orange inferno; walls of flame rather than tongues, a backdrop to silhouettes of slow moving men, any of whom might have been one of my uncles, creatures trying to communicate something to us, well aware of the lessons of darkness.

The steel industry 'died' (or was euthanised) in Sheffield in the 1970s and 80s. Most of the factories closed, and the jobs disappeared, though the output of steel actually increased. The few plants that remained in business required just a fraction of the labour, and nobody had much heart or desire to do anything but let the fabric of the old steel industry fall into ruin. A walk through Tinsley at that time, through empty streets, past abandoned, now superfluous, slabs of looming architecture, was to venture through a vast, eerie, magnificent industrial necropolis. The ruin and abandonment were depressing, and appalling in a way, but they were also spectacular, and of course many people could see the visual power of this. Local bands, often though not exclusively the purveyors of industrial music, the best known being Cabaret Voltaire and the Human League, used these easily available settings as locations in their videos. They looked great. By 1997 the ruin had become so picturesque that it could be used in *The Full Monty*, the hugely successful movie in which redundant steelworkers become strippers, though, as anyone might have objected, even to have had a job in the steel industry in Sheffield in 1997 from which to have been made redundant was a kind of fantasy.

And yet, despite the death of the industry on which Sheffield relied, the city never became an absolute ruin. It didn't become a complete, post-industrial wasteland. It never became a Detroit. The old steelworks were cleared away; the Don Valley became a place of sports arenas and retail parks. Four mighty cooling towers that had been visible alongside the M1 from the Tinsley Viaduct, giant concrete pig snouts poking out from smoke and fire, became much loved landmarks when they were about to be demolished, and the subject of a passionate though ultimately unsuccessful campaign to preserve them in some form or other, most probably as art objects.

These days when I go back to Sheffield I'm amazed at how prosperous so much of the city seems to be, and it's hard to think that the replacement of steel production by service and financial businesses has been such a terrible thing. Is there really anything better or nobler about working in a steel foundry as opposed to a call centre? Let China have their heavy industries, their pollution, their low safety standards, their short life-expectancy, their ruined cities and landscapes. In Sheffield people walk in the clean air, up and down its seven hills, you know, just like Rome.

* * *

Like anyone who has moved on and out from his hometown, I have a complicated relationship with the place. I knew I wanted to get out, and I did as soon as I reasonably could; I moved south, to be somewhere more 'metropolitan', whatever I thought that meant. And yet clearly I'm still attached to the place in a 'you can take the man out of Sheffield but you can't take Sheffield out of the man' kind of way. I'm not alone in this. Stephen Mallinder of Cabaret Voltaire, who spent a decade in Australia and is now an academic in Brighton, and the author of an essay titled 'Sheffield is not Sexy', tells me he still thinks of himself as a 'troublemaker from Walkley'.

I've written about the city, and about walking there, so it wasn't an absolute surprise when I got an offer to appear as an author at Sheffield's Off the Shelf Festival of Words. The organisers, of course, knew that I lived in Los Angeles, and while I was happy to be thought of as 'local lad makes good', I did wonder if there might be some element of 'local lad needs taking down a peg or two'. Just to make life more interesting, and perhaps more difficult, they wanted me to lead a walking tour of

Sheffield. It was the kind of invitation and challenge that I couldn't turn down, though the problems were obvious. It was decades since I'd lived in Sheffield full time. What kind of walk was I going to be able to do that would show Sheffield dwellers anything they didn't already know? I'm not much of a nostalgist, and I definitely didn't want to go the 'I remember when all this was fields' route.

So to make life even more complicated for myself, I decided I would first go for a walk in Los Angeles. Then some weeks later, accompanied by festival-goers, I'd go for a 'similar' walk in Sheffield. The idea was that the two routes should be, in certain respects, as similar to each other as possible: the same length, taking the same amount of time, walking the same 'shape' on the map of each city, and I decided that the two walks should be as 'circular' as possible, beginning and ending in the same place, and attempting to carve the circumference of a circle through the local geography.

I began with a map of Los Angeles, specifically of Hollywood, and I drew a circle on the map, using the very lowest-tech cartographical methods available – I drew a line around the base of a glass – and the plan was then to walk wherever that line took me. Of course there are very few cities where you can literally walk a circular route, and it's harder still in Los Angeles because of the streets' grid layout. Still, I plotted a route that was as close to circular as possible, though perhaps not really all that close, with a great many angles and sharp corners, but that was in the nature of the enterprise. The best-laid walking plans are always constrained and confounded by the situation on the ground: the map is not the territory.

The walk was arbitrary to some extent, and although it wasn't exactly a tourist route, I thought it was best to go by one or two places that people in Sheffield were likely to have heard of. So the walk touched on Sunset Boulevard, Hollywood Boulevard,

Vine Street, and it was a route that from time to time gave views of the Hollywood sign.

I walked the route more than once, and took photographs as I went, pictures that I would show to my tour group in Sheffield, things that struck me as typically Hollywood, but which I thought and hoped might have some equivalents in Sheffield, whether in an ironic sense or not. So I took pictures of palm trees, giant cacti, some cool old cars, a legal medical marijuana dispensary and, of course, of the Hollywood sign.

I went by the Capitol Records building – one of Hollywood's most famous 'programmatic' pieces of architecture, looking at least somewhat like a stack of seven-inch vinyl singles, if anyone knows what that is any more. I couldn't imagine a Sheffield equivalent for that. I photographed the mannequins in one of the stores on Hollywood Boulevard designed to satisfy all your stripper needs. I went by the Arclight, a movie theatre housed in a geodesic dome. I went by the Vedanta Temple, home of the Vedanta Church in Southern California – focusing on 'ultimate reality' – Christopher Isherwood was a big fan. That all seemed thoroughly Hollywood.

But the fact was, my taste for ruin was already running pretty high. I didn't quite have the nerve to poke around in the back alleys and abandoned buildings of Hollywood, and then do the same in Sheffield with my group of walkers, but a part of me wanted to. So I was happy enough that my route took me past some less than touristy sites, many of them adjacent to and in some cases under the Hollywood freeway.

I looked at the graffiti, the street art, the murals, tried not to spend too much time trying to define the differences between them: though surely the same issues of taxonomy would apply just as much in Sheffield, now that graffiti have become a universal language. I went by Pla-Boy Liquors located on one of the dodgiest, most crime-ridden corners in Hollywood. I also realised, though perhaps I'd known it all along, that Hollywood has a surprising amount of industrial architecture. The industry happens to be the movies rather than steel, but a warehouse or storage facility for movie equipment looks much like a warehouse or storage facility for anything else. And some of the architecture was in questionable shape, with barred and/or broken windows, crumbling stucco, flaking paint and rotten wood. I loved it.

Having done the Hollywood walk, I traced the shape of that route, now looking a good deal less circular, on a sheet of transparent plastic and placed it over a map of Sheffield. This would be the route I'd take at the Off the Shelf festival. Of course the geography of Sheffield, the layout of the streets, didn't conform to that of Hollywood, so the shape of the walk had to be modified again according to this new topography. The circle became ever less circular. I told myself this was just fine. In one sense I felt I might be over-prepared, trying too hard, but equally I couldn't escape the feeling that there was something absurd about the whole project. I hoped that was a good thing.

I arrived in Sheffield, the old home town, on Friday afternoon, with my map of the prospective route. I walked it that evening with my old Sheffield friend Steve, and it seemed to go well enough. There was no threat to life or limb; it wasn't unbearably dull. And then the next evening I walked it again, for 'real', for the Off the Shelf literary festival, in the dark, accompanied by an 'audience' of twenty-five or so fellow, paying, pedestrians. It felt odd to be paid to walk, and odder still that people would pay to walk with me. They were a likeable bunch, older rather than younger, some of them embarrassingly over-equipped as though in anticipation of some very serious hiking, others perhaps a little sullen, but it didn't look like a tough crowd; by and large I think literary walking tours don't attract the more unruly elements.

The differences between Sheffield and Hollywood hardly needed to be laboured, but finding the similarities was actually far easier than I imagined. For instance the walk began and ended at the Showroom Café Bar, squarely in the Cultural Industries Quarter, and it happened to be right opposite an endearingly eccentric piece of architecture that I knew fairly well, designed by Nigel Coates, consisting of four large metal-clad forms that are variously described as looking like drums, curling stones or crucibles; the last of these was the professed inspiration, English crucible steel being one of Sheffield's greatest inventions. Coates's building originally housed a rock 'n' roll museum, officially the National Centre for Popular Music, a pretty sad thing, which soon closed down, but rather than falling into ruin (which might have looked very cool indeed) it became the students' union for Sheffield Hallam University, and is known as The Hub.

In some sense then it's a programmatic building and it has something in common with the Capitol Records building in Hollywood: a stack of records for Hollywood, a steel-making crucible for Sheffield. I had immediately found an equivalent for the one thing I thought I never would. I even managed to find a Sheffield equivalent of the Hollywood sign (sort of), a large banner hung on a wall beside a piece of waste ground doing temporary service as a car park. The sign said, 'Welcome to Sheffield', though it seemed to me that whatever direction you were coming from you'd have been in Sheffield for some time before you received this welcome. The local people on the walk found this sign every bit as surprising as I did, and some said they'd never noticed it before, which made me feel pretty good.

I'd also been right about graffiti and street art. Sheffield was in the throes of its own street-art obsession. The most ubiquitous practitioner was one Kid Acne. His word pieces were all over the city, many of them simple messages painted big on the high boards surrounding empty plots of land: 'That'll Learn 'em', 'Dust in the Giant's Eye', 'Tha Knows', 'You'll Get What You're Given' and so on. He was also having a show in the Millennium Galleries, right next to the Ruskin Gallery, where the works were on canvas and paper rather than on the walls.

Of course street art has to make an immediate impression, but then it can hang around for a surprisingly long time. Just how many times can you read 'That'll Learn 'em' and still think it's interesting? Colin Drury, a columnist on the *Sheffield Star*, directed me towards an artist by the name of Phlegm, whose work was certainly more complex, and I imagine more enduring, though of course endurance may not be what everyone is looking for in street art. Phlegm at that time specialised in not quite human creatures, larger than 'life', long spindly, elongated black-and-white figures, their faces frequently hidden or hooded, often carrying outsized telescopes. These characters, playful and spooky, not exactly sinister but by no means entirely benign, loomed over us at various points along the walk. They were often painted on boards rather than directly on to walls, and it came as a surprise to me that nobody had unscrewed the boards and taken possession of the artworks. They would have if it had been Banksy.

And if graffiti were blooming amid the neglected buildings, so too was nature; the other countryside. Close to the city centre there was an area that had been readied for redevelopment a few years back. It had been given a new name, actually two new names, Sevenstone or the New Retail Quarter (at the last count Sheffield had eleven 'quarters'). The project had come with all the usual promises and vocabulary of regeneration: public/private partnership, improved infrastructure, mixed use, leisure facilities. It had involved the compulsory purchase of various sites, and some buildings had been shuttered and labelled with Dangerous Structure signs, and in a few cases already

demolished. But then financial reality had set in, progress had stopped, the money had evaporated, leaving, according to the *Sheffield Star*, a 'swath of derelict land and blighted buildings around the city centre', though frankly it wasn't nearly as good as that sounds.

Still, there was one large impressive square of empty land, hemmed in on two sides by rough, mottled, windowless walls, on the other two by metal fencing, where an explosion of buddleia had burst out as if from a bomb-site. And right next door there was the back entrance to a pub, the Cutler. They hadn't put a lot of effort into sprucing up the rear, and the sign above the entrance simply read 'the utler'. There was an empty car park opposite, and in the daytime it had seemed unremarkable enough, but now at night, as I took my charges past it, it looked alive under the glint of the streetlights. We saw that the customers of the pub had found the car park a convenient place to hurl and smash their empty glasses and bottles; an objectionable and anti-social practice for sure, but in this light, on this night, with the dull, smooth sheen of the tarmac beneath the sparkling, jagged layer of thin, evenly-spread glass shards, it looked absolutely wonderful, absolutely beautiful.

I'm not sure if any of the other walkers thought this was the highlight of the tour, though I think one possibly might have, a Dutch graduate student of landscape architecture who asked a lot of questions about parking that I couldn't answer, but of course I certainly did. Having thought about it since I reckon it was because this was a moment, a sight, a situation, that in one sense had very little to do with me. I hadn't planned or organised it, hadn't even noticed it in the daylight, and it wasn't the reason any of us were there. On the other hand if this event of mine hadn't taken place, if I hadn't conducted this Hollywood–Sheffield, twin-centered circular walk, none of us would ever have seen it at all.

Afterwards there were questions and answers back in the Showroom Café Bar and it seemed that my guided walk had been a success. The only time I saw people's eyes glaze over was when I started to talk about psychogeography.

* * *

Writers are simple, if over-imaginative, creatures, and there's always the fantasy that after a literary event the author will be whisked away on some wild, out-of-character, disreputable, manic joyride. In my admittedly limited experience this very, very rarely happens. More often you end up alone in your hotel room, glass of over-priced wine in hand, experiencing both exhilaration and anticlimax.

In particularly anticlimactic mode I stared out of the sealed hotel window and looked up and out at the vast, looming architectural folly of Park Hill, Sheffield's set of brutalist deck-access flats, once the most undesirable of council housing, now a Grade II listed building and securely in the private sector. Nikolaus Pevsner, writing in 1967, said it would 'be a slum in half a century or less' and in fact it took *considerably* less. The flats appeared in the Human League's video for 'Being Boiled', made in the late seventies, as a convincing stand-in for totalitarian, futuristic, possibly Soviet architecture. Even in the Socialist Republic of South Yorkshire, we weren't very keen on that kind of thing.

When I was growing up, Park Hill was notorious as a place where outsiders were advised not to set foot. A boy had been killed walking past when somebody had hurled a television set off one of the upper concrete decks and scored a direct hit on his head. Now, as I looked out of the hotel I could see there was a banner strung across the flats, and could read the words 'Park Hill I Love You' in faux graffiti-style lettering. In the morning I would see that the full message read 'Park Hill I Love You Will You Marry Me?', a reference to a famous graffito sprayed on a nearby bridge by some desperate suitor in 2001. It was now being used as an advertising slogan to sell the flats, or 'homes and workspaces' as the developer would have it.

The hotel was in a part of Sheffield I'd never even heard of, certainly not one of the places celebrated in song by Jarvis Cocker, a regenerated area known as the Victoria Quays. I think it used to be called the Sheffield Canal Basin, if it was called anything. The whole area was now extensively, though not completely, cleaned up, and not a bad place to do a certain kind of post-industrial walking, which I proceeded to do next morning, and if I happened to run into some genuine ruin, then so much the better.

The area had no doubt got its new name because it was adjacent to where the old Sheffield Victoria Railway Station used to be. I certainly went to the station a few times as a kid, both as a passenger with my parents, and on at least one ill-fated outing with some trainspotters from my school. I never really 'got' trainspotting, though I did develop an uninformed, largely undifferentiated enthusiasm for trains, tracks and railway buildings, which remains with me. I knew that the old Victoria Station had been demolished some time ago, but even so I walked around looking for signs of it. I could find hardly any, could barely imagine where it had once stood. There was still a station hotel and there was a trackless railway viaduct (not nearly as grand or picturesque as the one in Monsal Dale), but even so, it took quite an exercise of the imagination to picture where the station had once been. It seemed simply to have disappeared. We are accustomed to change and decay in all around we see, but here there had been a lot of the former and rather little of the latter. I thought it my duty to find some pockets of disorder and decay, places where the best efforts of public and private enterprise hadn't quite battened down the hatches.

There were some very presentable houseboats on the water right outside the hotel, but a little farther along the canal things looked more careworn, less decorative: there were buildings with bricked-up windows, a rusting iron bridge, and under the disused railways arches there was all kinds of mess. In another age you would have thought that somebody had simply dumped a lot of rubbish there, piles of paper, wood and glass, and even an old bus. Back then it would have been junk or, at best, scrap, but now this place was designated, or at least named, a recycling facility. These heaps of detritus were all about reclamation and repurposing, and only a churl such as myself would have thought they had anything to do with ruin.

* * *

In the afternoon Steve and I took a stroll in the Sheffield General Cemetery, saw the abandoned chapel, the overgrown gravestones, the faceless and headless statuary, a mausoleum that was a pretty decent replica of Rome's second-century-BC Temple of Portunus. If this sounds unlikely, bear in mind that the grounds of Halswell House in Somerset also have a folly version of that temple, built in the eighteenth century and restored in the 1990s, having fallen into ruin and having been used as a cattleshed. And finally we hopped over some barbed wire and poked about outside the bricked-up catacombs, where we met a drunk man with an Eastern European accent who told us to be careful, he'd once fallen into a hole up there.

We also went to Peveril Castle, in Castelton, a medieval chunk that featured in a Walter Scott novel; it looks today like a giant decayed molar, sitting on top of a steep limestone hill, dauntingly high above the town and quite a challenge to get to even for an enthusiastic ruin walker. And as we were driving home Steve showed me various sights and changes in Sheffield. He was as keen as I'd been to avoid the 'I remember when all this was fields' approach. However, as we drove along Prince of Wales Road, a route I used to know pretty well, he pointed out a large open green space, as big as many a city park, that had once been part of a densely populated council estate, the Manor. Hundreds of houses had gone, and had never been replaced. This allowed Steve to say, 'I remember when these fields were all houses.' We both enjoyed that.

It was getting dark and starting to rain, and we said we'd go and explore this area some other time, when I was next in Sheffield. And so, just over a year later, right before my next visit, Steve sent me a link to a story on the *Daily Mirror* website from 2007 headlined 'This is Our Manor', written by a journalist named Julie McCaffrey. This alarmist bit of writing began with a taxi driver refusing to take her to the Manor. 'Not worth the muggings,' he had said. The piece reported an RAC breakdown mechanic being assaulted there, the pelting of firemen, a milkman being stabbed to death and a twenty-seven-year-old woman having her head stomped on by a gang while her daughter and nephew cowered behind a wall.

Still, our intrepid reporter got there one way or another, where she encountered a lad smashing bottles with a cricket bat, heard rap music issuing from houses, and was regaled with reports of old ladies being called miserable c——s. She also found 'fifty-nine-year-old George', who said, 'Thirty-five years ago there wasn't a better estate in Sheffield.' George, I was in Sheffield thirty-five years ago, and trust me there were much better estates.

As I grew up in Sheffield, the perceived gradations of status and quality among council estates were sometimes arcane, and seldom objectively provable, but always clear. Longley where my parents lived was middling, not as good as Norfolk Park, but always better than the Manor which was know to be 'rough', although when we went to visit Auntie Mary and Uncle Ken, who lived there, I often wandered the streets, either alone or with my cousin Sylvia, and I never saw anything even vaguely resembling trouble. I never found anything very interesting either.

The newspaper report sounded surprising, but also potentially encouraging. A visit to the Manor sounded like the stuff of adventure and reportage and a certain amount of low-level risk. Steve had recently bought a new car and was worried this might be a provocation to the feral lads of the estate, but hell, it would be worth it for a story – besides which, I had the nagging feeling that perhaps you couldn't absolutely believe every word you read in the *Daily Mirror*.

Who knew how things would be when we got there? But one question arose, something that had never crossed my mind in all the long years I'd been familiar with Sheffield: why exactly was a council estate called the Manor? Well, as with Frecheville and Wombwell, the name itself is easily explained. In the early part of the sixteenth century George Talbot, the 4th Earl of Shrewsbury, built a lodge there, a country retreat within the boundaries of what was an extremely large deer park. The place was variously known as Sheffield Manor, Manor Lodge or Manor Castle. The name came to describe the whole area.

Cardinal Wolsey was accommodated for eighteen days in what became known as Wolsey's Tower, while he was on his way to London, for an audience with Henry VIII which would almost certainly have resulted in his death; but he only made it as far as Leicester. Mary, Queen of Scots was held prisoner there by the 6th Earl, also named George Talbot, and one of the husbands of Bess of Hardwick, of whom more later. The property was later owned by the Duke of Norfolk, who didn't take much interest in it. He let it fall into ruin and eventually sold it to the tenant farmers. Some of the stonework was sold off as building material, and the former tenants built cottages inside the remaining, ruined walls.

This was news to me. My childhood and youth were not so much sheltered as steeped in ignorance. I knew a little about the great houses around Sheffield: Chatsworth, Haddon Hall, Hardwick Hall, but our family had never visited any of them, so it was hardly surprising that Sheffield Manor and its ruins had passed me by completely. And perhaps this was also because back in the day it had simply been regarded as a ruin. Now it was part of Sheffield's 'heritage'. The Turret House, where Mary had been incarcerated, and the only part now *not* in ruins, is a listed building, and the whole site has been declared both a 'scheduled ancient monument' and a 'site of National Heritage Significance'. A million pounds of lottery money has been poured in, and a remarkably named organisation WREN (it stands for Waste Recycling Environmental Limited) has funded (I'm not making any of this up) a 'Romantic Ruins' project, which included the creation of various historic gardens and green spaces in and around the ruined structures.

It seemed compulsory that we see the ruins of the old manor before we saw the ruins of the council estate sharing its name. So off we went, and yes, you could certainly see what they meant by romantic. The crumbling walls and partly demolished structures pierced by glassless, frameless windows did have a grace and elegance about them. Sturdy stone chimneys rose above it all, and historically accurate gardens had been planted at ground level. By the visitors' centre there was a free-standing section of wall with a low-topped archway where the ivy had been allowed, or encouraged, to grow. It would have been absolutely at home in any Augustan landscape. It all looked great, and it would be churlish, and not even all that accurate, to object to any of this on the grounds of inauthenticity.

But call me perverse, the thing I remember best about the Manor ruins is the privy adjacent to Wolsey's Tower, 'Wolsey's garderobe' if you wanted to give it a period flavour, now open to the elements since one of its walls has gone. In fact it looked like one of those double privies where a couple of users could sit side by side, though presumably Wolsey was allowed his privacy. But even if it must have been more secluded at one time, the bare stonework couldn't have been much less chilly or inhospitable. When Wolsey was in his tower, he was seriously ill, either from natural causes or because he'd poisoned himself knowing what was to come when and if he got to London. So he may well have had much business in the privy. But now there was a new inhabitant in there, a twitchy, earth-coloured shrew that scurried around determinedly, all business, down in the dirt floor, unaware of the historic significance of the place he was in, unaware and indifferent to the fact that he was living in a ruin, much less a romantic one.

And then on to the council estate of the same name, to the wide open ruined spaces where the council houses used to be. I knew why the houses had been demolished. It was because they'd been built using something known as black mortar, more correctly black-ash mortar, a cheap material containing ash or clinker, a by-product from power stations, of which there were plenty around Sheffield. Wall ties are the metal connectors set

in the mortar to hold the bricks and walls together, but black ash is corrosive and caused the ties to deteriorate and eventually fail. Horizontal cracks started appearing in the walls, and the usual solution would be to repoint the brickwork, simultaneously taking out all the old ties and replacing them with stainless steel. But the Sheffield Council decided it was cheaper and easier to demolish the houses and rehouse the tenants. Part of my father's job when he worked for the council had been to go around explaining to people why they had to leave their homes and be relocated at the council's whim: a hardship posting if ever there was one.

And so in certain enclaves of the Manor estate, the black mortar houses had gone, never to be replaced, and that accounted for the large expanse of open territory we'd seen a year earlier, and to which we now returned. Steve parked his new car in what he thought looked like a safe place and we set off walking.

On the ground, the impression was not so much that the houses had been demolished, but rather that they might have been simply vaporised. The layout remained: roads, pavements, a traffic island, were all still there, but there was absolutely no sign of the houses; no rubble, no foundations, no architectural footprint. In fact the roads were laid out geometrically, in circles, ovals, concentric curves, with some streets radiating like spokes, as though somebody in the Sheffield Planning Department had been looking at Le Corbusier's Radiant City and decided it could use a few curves. The effect here on the Manor was ghostly, uncomfortable, these roads to nowhere were distinctly unsettling. They also seemed too small, too close together, more like a model than a real territory, like one of those carpets for a child's bedroom, with roads and crossings and traffic islands jostling on top of each other.

We walked along these bare roads, across a wide, open, utterly uninhabited space. It wasn't entirely bleak. There was thick grass all around us – it had been a wet summer – but there were absolutely no people. We saw a few scattered, broken plastic toys, some beer cans, a puddle of broken glass, a fallen concrete bollard that was too short and stubby ever to have been genuinely totemic. Even so, given the size of the place, it was much freer of junk and detritus than anyone could have reasonably expected.

There were metal barriers across the ends of some of the roads, to prevent cars and trucks from being driven along them: in the past the Manor had a reputation as a place where joyriders came and raced their stolen cars then dumped them and set them on fire. There was no sign of any of that now, though it seemed that any self-respecting joyrider would have had no trouble whatsoever simply driving on the grass, and going round the barriers. Maybe nobody ever came here.

There was, however, a single structure that remained amid the grassy expanse, a brick-built cube, a little smaller than a single-car garage, with two heavy louvred doors in the front. I assumed it had to be something to do with electricity, a small substation perhaps. It had one of those yellow triangles showing a stick man being hit with a bolt of lightning, and there were a couple of signs on the walls warning that anti-climb paint had been 'applied'. That may have stopped the climbing but it hadn't stopped some half-hearted graffiti, chiefly the number 253. If this was an indication of gang affiliation I haven't been able to find out the nature of the gang.

However, as with the free-standing section of wall in the grounds of Manor Lodge, this brick cube was weighed down under a mantle of ivy, giving the effect of great age, maybe even of romance. Despite it being a lone conspicuous structure it looked perfectly at home, like it had always been there And it was, of course, in one sense a domestic enough structure, some part of the process by which power was delivered to people's homes. But in another sense it didn't look very domestic at all. Steve and I had seen enough old-school science-fiction movies to think that its ordinariness was bogus, all part of the plan, that this could be a base from which the alien life forms, the robots, maybe even the Martians, would emerge to become our overlords. It also occurred to us that it might be a place where the bad lads of the Manor estate might lurk, ready to leap out on a couple of passing strangers. The cube was pretty much at the centre of the open space, and the inhabitants would surely be faster runners than us, and there was always the question of Steve's back and the sciatica. We'd be easy meat.

Well it didn't happen, naturally. Feral lads, unlike alien life forms, are perhaps not known for their patience. It would be a long wait before they got anything that resembled prey. There really was nobody around. We could see one or two walkers over on the far side of the space where some of the non-black-mortar houses still stood, but they were hundreds of yards away. Where we were, nobody walked, nobody was hanging around, nobody was playing football, certainly nobody was breaking bottles with a cricket bat, not even was anybody exercising their dog. Until, at last, inevitably, some figures appeared on the horizon.

It was a small group of people walking towards us: two women, a small boy, and a man carrying a baby; hardly the wild boys of our imaginations. They were walking determinedly, not just out for stroll, trying to get somewhere, or perhaps get back from somewhere. There was something ragged and windblown about them, a morning-afterish aura, even though it was late afternoon.

As they got closer I realised they were much younger than I'd thought. The two women were girls in their mid-teens, the man only a little older. None of them looked old enough to be the parent of the small boy, though I suppose any of them could have been a parent of the baby. The two girls were dressed up as though they might have been to a party. They were wearing black dresses, cocktail dresses it seemed to me, shiny fabric, shoulderless in one case, and they sported very high heels, though one of them was carrying hers and walking barefoot. Later I wondered if maybe they'd been to a wedding or a funeral, the time of day was probably about right for the latter, and they did seem a bit glum.

They looked at us with understandable suspicion. Two men of a certain age with nothing better to do on a weekday afternoon, walking, standing around, looking, talking, pointing, taking photographs. What did they think we were? A couple of blokes from the council, surveyors, social workers, do-gooders? I'm pretty sure they couldn't have thought we were coppers. The true story, that I was a writer from Sheffield, now based in Los Angeles, there to take a look at the ruins of a place I used to know, seemed the least probable.

I didn't expect a meeting of minds between us and them, but since their walking route was about to cross ours, it seemed only reasonable to acknowledge their existence, say something. 'All right?' I said gently to one of the girls. She looked at me sadly, and nodded in what was not quite assent. I got the feeling that things were not really all right.

*   *   *

To round off our trip, so that we felt utterly immersed in ruin, Steve and I went to Hardwick Hall, just a few miles outside Sheffield, built by Bess of Hardwick in the late sixteenth century, after the death of her fourth husband George Talbot, he of Sheffield Manor and Mary Queen of Scots fame. I've always had a considerable, if grudging, admiration for Bess. I suspect few people in the history of England have ever married 'better' than she did. There were four husbands, none married for love as far as one can tell, and she survived them all, picking up fortunes from each of them to become the second richest women in England, after Queen Elizabeth I.

She was sometimes known as Building Bess, because of her architectural enthusiasm, self-aggrandising as it was. She was partly responsible for Chatsworth House, which still regularly polls as one of Britain's favourite stately homes, and is still thoroughly intact, though there is a ruined mill in the surrounding parkland. In fact Bess built two Hardwick Halls, which was why Steve and I were going there. She built the pair more or less simultaneously, or at least she started building the second before the first was finished. These days the New Hall, the marginally later of the two, remains in pretty good shape, another much visited attraction, and a fine example of English Renaissance architecture, with a grand and impressive façade, 'more window than wall', bearing Bess's initials (E. S. for Elizabeth Shrewsbury) in four places on the roofline. The other Hardwick Hall lies in ruin. This is actually a little more reasonable and comprehensible than it might sound.

Bess was in her late sixties when she started building what is now known as the Old Hall. She was bitterly estranged from her fourth husband, George Talbot, and they lived apart, so naturally she felt the need to build a grand new home for herself. She had sufficient funds to transform her father's comparatively modest ancestral manor house into a much grander country house and began to do so in 1587. But then in 1590, as work continued, Talbot died and Bess suddenly inherited the funds to build something much grander still: the New Hall.

Some think she may have intended the two buildings to exist and operate together, side by side, like a pair of unmatching wings of a single structure, though the architect of the New Hall, Robert Smythson, would surely have been severely miffed by this idea: his grand scheme yoked to someone else's lesser work. And in any case, although the two buildings are indeed very close together they don't lie in a relation that would make any obvious sense as 'wings'. The Old Hall was completed in 1596, the New Hall a year later. Bess, now in her seventies, was able to enjoy them both for a little over a decade, until her death in 1608.

After that, her son and his heirs preferred to live in the even grander Chatsworth House, not so far away, though both the Hardwick Halls remained in liveable condition until the 1750s, when the Old Hall was partly demolished, or perhaps we should say dismantled. Scholars differ, and although parts of the hall were certainly sold off for cash, it's not clear if this was done simply because of the need for funds, or more intriguingly, so that the Old Hall would become a folly ruin visible from the New Hall.

The two things are by no means mutually exclusive, but I can't help thinking that any serious eighteenth-century landscape architect would have dismantled the Old Hall in a much more organised and 'romantic' way. The ruins are picturesque to a degree but as garden follies go it's hugely out of scale for the site, massive, four storeys high, and from certain angles it's a giant, looming hulk. If you view it from the side lawn of the New Hall you see a huge, four-square slab of masonry, pierced with mighty rectangular holes where the windows used to be. The effect seems, to a modern eye anyway, that of a brooding Gothic presence rather than a decorative one, dominating the view rather than enhancing it, and sometimes blocking it completely.

Today large parts of the Old Hall are roofless and floorless, and even though the structure has been made safe and secure for visitors, you don't have to be a complete wimp to feel a twinge of nervousness as you climb the open wooden stairs; and when you get up to the very top, to roof level, and look out across the landscape to see the M1 carving its way through the Derbyshire hills, allowing fools to get from London to Leeds and many places in between, and then look down all the way through the core of the building, to the dirt floor of the kitchen, seventy-five or eighty feet below, well a stab of vertigo seems the most natural thing in the world.

Despite the many absences of such things as wainscoting, floorboards, glass, there is still some very elaborate plasterwork in place. No doubt it would have been too difficult to move or sell off, but it still seems remarkable that it's survived the rigours of so many Derbyshire winters. I was standing, staring, admiring a particularly fine plasterwork frieze above one of the fireplaces on the top floor, when a woman beside me said, loudly and enthusiastically, 'Ooh, it's just like Abu Simbel.'

She wasn't talking to me, but to her husband, who was standing glumly beside her. I'm generally resistant to regional stereotyping but here was a man who seemed to be working pretty hard to present himself as a blunt, no-nonsense northerner. He grunted emptily. I wasn't sure whether he didn't know what she was talking about, whether he knew but disagreed, or whether he simply didn't care. My money would be on the last of these.

'You know,' she insisted. 'Abu Simbel, in Egypt.'

This time the husband didn't even grunt.

I assumed she was talking about the frieze I was looking at. It was impressive. If I'd had to guess there and then, I'd have assumed it showed two Roman soldiers (one without a head) with Cupid between them, but I now know that, according to some sources anyway, it depicts the giants Gog and Magog, rather reduced in size if they're in fact giants, and that the figure between them is an allegorical depiction of Desire. Other sources suggest the winged figure is Patience, and was copied, at Bess's instructions, from an engraving showing the triumph of Patience over Fortune, a notion she might have found especially resonant, but not necessarily. Yes, it does take a lot of patience to outlive four husbands, but surely good luck has quite a lot to do with it as well.

Abu Simbel is the complex of temples on the shores of Lake Nasser, moved wholesale to higher ground when rising waters caused by the building of the Aswan Dam threatened their very existence. The Great Temple indeed has some imposing statues, though carved out of rock rather than plaster, depicting Rameses II (aka Ozymandias), Queen Nefertiti and various princes and princesses. They come in different scales and sizes, but in general they're colossal, some of them easily as high as the Old Hall. The whole thing is topped by a row of carved baboons, regarded as protectors of water.

Is this really what the woman meant, that Gog and Magog resemble Rameses and Nefertiti, that the figures in a plaster frieze above a fireplace in Derbyshire resemble eighty-foot-tall Egyptian rock carvings? It seems quite a stretch. But maybe she meant that all ruins looked pretty much alike to her. That sounds reductive, I know, but she didn't seem to mean it in a bored or dismissive way. She was genuinely enthusiastic about what she was looking at. The excitement with which she spoke seemed to indicate that she loved the resemblance, the correlation, and that she too was a lover of ruin in all its forms. There are a lot of us about, on the streets of Sheffield as much as in Hardwick Hall, as much as in Abu Simbel. I can see, however, how our shared enthusiasm is lost on the likes of her husband.

And I'm also left uncertain about what Ruskin would have thought. Yes he loved ruins, and he loved architecture that showed wear and patina. But I don't know that he'd have been especially happy to see the two structures at Hardwick; one a preserved ruin, one a restored country house. Restoration would have been the big problem. In *The Lamp of Memory* he writes:

> Do not let us talk then of restoration. The thing is a Lie from beginning to end. You may make a model of a building as you may of a corpse, and your model may have the shell of the old walls within it as your cast might have the skeleton, with what advantage I neither see nor care; but the old building is destroyed, and that more totally and mercilessly than if it had sunk into a heap of dust, or melted into a mass of clay. If [there is a necessity, it] is a necessity for destruction. Accept it as such, pull the building down, throw its stones into neglected corners, make ballast of them, or mortar, if you will; but do it honestly, and do not set up a Lie in their place.

I'm guessing he'd have been pretty happy about the wide open spaces of the Manor council estate.

5

Some Desert Ruins

> One of the reasons that the proposition 'the desert is where God is and man is not' does not mean much to me is that, puzzled to know what I'm doing in the desert, I hope to find illumination by the study of what other men have been doing in the desert, why they did it, and why they thought it proper to do so.
>
> Reyner Banham, *Scenes in America Deserta*

Los Angeles, of course, is perfectly capable of ruining itself without need of natural disasters, terrorists or celebrity architects. For a city with a comparatively short history it has a rich tradition of civil disturbance and riot. Most have had a racial component, and often involved sins of commission or omission by the police: the Chinese riot and massacre of 1871 – five hundred white men attacking, robbing and eventually murdering Chinese immigrants while the cops looked on; the Zoot Suits Riots of 1943 – white servicemen versus Latino youth; the Rodney King riots of 1992, following the acquittal of the cops who beat King after a hundred-mile-an-hour car chase – fifty-three deaths, two thousand injured, a billion dollars' worth of damage.

By the Rodney King standards, the Watts Riots of 1965 were small potatoes, 'only' thirty-four deaths, only a thousand and thirty-two injuries, only forty million dollar's worth of property damage. What gives the Watts Riots special status is the fact that in some quarters they're known as the Watts Rebellion or the Watts Insurrection. The language of revolutionary politics sits a little uneasily here if you ask me. Just how 'revolutionary' was it to toss petrol bombs into convenience stores, or to loot the row of shops along 103rd Street, the neighbourhood's main shopping area, before setting fire to the buildings and transforming the street into what became known as Charcoal Alley?

Some, naturally, were perfectly content with a Marxist analysis. One was Guy Debord: Monsieur Psychogeography himself. In an essay titled 'The Decline and Fall of the Spectacle-Commodity Economy' (feeling weary already?) he offered the opinion that:

> The Los Angeles rebellion was a rebellion against the commodity, against the world of the commodity in which worker-consumers are hierarchically subordinated to commodity standards . . . The Los Angeles blacks take modern capitalist propaganda, its publicity of abundance, literally. They want to possess now all the objects shown and abstractly accessible, because they want to use them. In this way they are challenging their exchange-value . . . But once the vaunted abundance is taken at face value and directly seized, instead of being eternally pursued in the rat-race of alienated labor and increasingly unmet social needs, real desires begin to be expressed in festive celebration, in playful self-assertion, in the potlatch of destruction. People who destroy commodities show their human superiority over commodities.

Well, this would be a lot more persuasive if the 'rebels' hadn't loaded up with appliances before torching the bourgeois emporia that sold them. Still, I think it's fair to say that one man who would have understood Debord's rhetoric even as he rejected it, was the artist Noah Purifoy. Purifoy, an African-American, had trained as a teacher and social worker in the 1940s, before studying fine art at Chouinard Art Institute in the mid 1950s. He described his experience of the riots like this:

> Judson [Powell] and I, while teaching at the Watts Tower Art Center, watched aghast the rioting, looting and burning during the August happening. And while the debris was still smoldering, we ventured into the rubble like other junkers of the community, digging and searching, but unlike others, obsessed without quite knowing why . . . we gave much thought to the oddity of our found things.

At that moment, either by default or by some deep instinct, Noah Purifoy became a maker of assemblage art. Prior to the riots he had worked as a window dresser and furniture designer, and by his own account was materially well off. After the Watts Riots he took a self-imposed vow of poverty, both in his personal life and in the art materials he used, and this could well be seen as a personal revolution. Deciding to use junk as your medium is a political as much as an aesthetic choice.

About a year after the riots, some of the work Purifoy created from the debris appeared in a group show later known as *66 Signs of Neon*, part of the Simon Rodia Commemorative Watts Renaissance of the Arts Festival: Rodia had died about a month before the riots. The work was shown not in a gallery but at Markham Junior High School.

As it happened, a young writer who was enjoying some success with his first two novels, went to Watts at that time on a journalistic assignment from the *New York Times*. The writer's name was Thomas Pynchon. The piece he wrote was 'A Journey to the Mind of Watts' and it was published in the *New York Times Magazine* in June 1966. He observed the chaos and destruction still visible on the streets, and wrote:

> A kid could come along in his bare feet and step on this

> glass – not that you'd ever know. These kids are so tough you can pull slivers of it out of them and never get a whimper. It's part of their landscape, both the real and the emotional one: busted glass, busted crockery, nails, tin cans, all kinds of scrap and waste. Traditionally Watts. An Italian immigrant named Simon Rodia spent 30 years gathering some of it up and converting a little piece of the neighborhood along 107th Street into the famous Watts Towers . . . a fantasy of fountains, boats, tall openwork spires, encrusted with a dazzling mosaic of Watts debris. Next to the Towers, along the old Pacific Electric tracks, kids are busy every day busting more bottles on the street rails. But Simon Rodia is dead, and now the junk just accumulates.

Well only up to a point.

In due course Pynchon did see the exhibition in Markham Junior High, and found

> a roomful of sculptures fashioned entirely from found objects – found, symbolically enough, and in the Simon Rodia tradition, among the wreckage the rioting had left. Exploiting textures of charred wood, twisted metal, fused glass, many of the works were fine, honest rebirths.
>
> In one corner was this old, busted, hollow TV set with a rabbit-ears antenna on top; inside where its picture tube should have been, gazing out with scorched wiring threaded like electronic ivy among its crevices and sockets, was a human skull. The name of the piece was *The Late, Late, Late Show.*

It's not clear whether that piece was by Purifoy or not, Pynchon doesn't mention Purifoy by name, and the piece doesn't appear in the exhibition catalogue, but it certainly sounds like it might have been a Purifoy. The exhibition toured the United States for quite a few years, but no permanent home could be found for it, and in due course most of the elements returned to the Pynchonian entropy from which they had come, although a piece did re-emerge in one of the exhibitions in the series Pacific Standard Time, in LA in 2011/12.

* * *

As an aside, readers of Pynchon's *Gravity's Rainbow* may well recall the Poisson formula or Poisson distribution, named for Siméon Denis Poisson, a French mathematician and physicist, born in 1741. It's part of probability theory, used to determine the likelihood of certain events occurring in a given time frame. It can therefore tell us whether events that actually do happen are truly or only apparently random. In the case of Pynchon's novel, the probability in question is the distribution of V2 rockets raining destruction on London towards the end of World War II.

Poisson first published his work in the late eighteenth century, but in the early twentieth a Swedish actuary named Filip Lundberg took the tenets of Poisson distribution and applied them to the insurance industry. He called his discovery – and this is almost too good – 'ruin theory', its purpose being to determine, in actuarial terms, the probability of the 'ultimate ruin' of a given system.

Incidentally, Guy Debord's essay did report that when the California authorities declared the Watts Riots a 'state of insurrection', the insurance companies with liabilities in Watts were able to claim that their policies didn't cover risks at that level.

* * *

Post-1966, Noah Purifoy had a career that will be familiar to many accomplished but commercially not so successful artists. For a long period he seems to have put more energy into facilitating other people's creativity than into expressing his own. He taught and served on the Watts Arts Council, while continuing to have work in group shows. It was only in the late 1980s and more especially the 1990s that his reputation really took off and he became much more widely known and celebrated. Suddenly, though it might not have seemed so sudden from his point of view, he was having one-man exhibitions, receiving grants from the likes of the Warhol Foundation, getting work into museums' permanent collections, and having both scholarly and popular articles written about him.

This coincided, though it was hardly a coincidence, with his leaving Los Angeles to live in Joshua Tree, in the Mojave Desert. He made the move in 1989 when he was in his early seventies. There, a few miles out of town, down a dirt road or two, he had a trailer plus two and a half acres, and eventually ten acres thanks to a contribution from Ed Ruscha, and he turned the land into a sculpture park filled with his own assemblage art. Purifoy died in 2004 and what remains, which is plenty, is now the Noah Purifoy Outdoor Desert Art Museum of Assemblage Sculpture.

It must once have been a very difficult place to find, and the Purifoy Foundation website still doesn't offer the address, but in the age of blogging, Google Maps and TripAdvisor (for God's sake), any damn fool can find his way there. And so off I went to see Noah Purifoy's ten acres of desert and walk among his sculptures.

There are, I think, big risks in being an assemblage artist. Unless you're a Rauschenberg or a Duchamp, it's hard to make assemblage art that doesn't look a lot like everybody else's assemblage art, and certainly the components, the vocabulary if you like, of Purifoy's art are familiar enough: old TV sets and computers, bowling balls, lavatory pans, stuffed toy animals, bicycles and so on. What distinguishes Purifoy's art is the scale, the intensity, the wit, a sort of kindliness, a lack of overt aggression even though some of the work is directly concerned with death and racism. And above all there's the setting.

However good a piece of sculpture is, it'll almost certainly look better in the middle of the desert: the clear light, lots of space around it, a deep blue backdrop of sky, a low cholla cactus lurking in front of it, a giant, jagged Joshua tree rising behind. And there really is a *lot* of art there in Noah Purifoy's outdoor museum. When you first see it from a distance, it looks incredibly busy, a series of strewn, diverse structures, not exactly harmonious, and without an obvious overall design. You see a lot of strong, tall verticals, things that look like totem poles, things that look like space rockets, constructions made of car parts, a kind of gateway built of tyres. The effect is of an abandoned campsite, or perhaps a recently vacated ghost town, or a ruined art gallery without walls, floors or ceilings. There's no entry charge, and apparently no custodian. There wasn't even a boundary fence, and that's the way Purifoy wanted it, though I understand the Foundation is contemplating putting one in as a basic security measure.

As you step, eagerly but gingerly, across the sandy dirt road on to the identical sandy dirt of the Purifoy lot, it feels even more like walking into a ruined city, because quite a few of the pieces do resemble buildings. There are various shacks, a deconstructed Quonset hut, some free-standing walls, a ramshackle open-air theatre, a piece called *The White House* which was originally called *The Castle*, and one is even named *Homage to Frank Gehry* (a corrugated-metal construction that has at least some resemblance to Gehry's house in Santa Monica). Amid all this is also the trailer that Purifoy called home.

Many pieces, however, don't resemble buildings in any way: there's a piece that looks like a stretch of railway line with vacuum cleaners and Heath Robinson contraptions instead of carriages, there's a faux graveyard and an earthwork – a deep hole in the ground with a wooden bridge across it.

None of this stuff is in the very best shape because the extreme climate of the Mojave Desert doesn't do much to preserve things in their original state; some of the pieces tilt alarmingly, straining against the metal cords that try to keep them in place. The sheets of corrugated metal lining the earthwork have come adrift, and the wooden bridge is falling apart. There are Danger and Keep Out signs at either end of it, but it's an unnecessary warning: only a damned fool would think of walking across it.

You begin to wonder how this stuff looked when it was first constructed. Surely it was never 'pristine'. The materials from which it was made were already, in Pynchon's term, busted. Surely it must always have had a look of mess and decay? Weren't these 'buildings' in ruin even as they were being built? It's a notion that's only reinforced by Purifoy's much quoted remark, 'I do assemblage. I don't do maintenance.' If you don't do maintenance, things fall into ruin that much more quickly.

Even quite recent photographs of the place show it in a significantly different state from the way it looked when I saw it. And I imagine that it changes every day – there's constant slippage, things shifting and tumbling, even as volunteers come in to patch things up. Purifoy seems not to have objected to other people doing maintenance on his behalf.

The Purifoy Foundation is trying to conserve the works, which must be a very tricky and downright paradoxical enterprise. Yes, it would be terrible if all this were to fall apart or disappear, and yet ruin, corrosion and collapse seem to be an integral part of the grand plan. Purifoy's work is process as much as finished object. It seems an unresolvable problem, and I suppose some kind of benign neglect would be the best solution, but getting the right balance between neglect and benignity will require some extraordinarily fine calibration.

As well as the 'finished' works of art, there were also piles of junk or scrap still lying around. In many ways these piles of junk inside the boundaries of the sculpture park weren't so very different from the piles of junk you might find anywhere else in the desert, but these had the distinction of being the raw materials that Purifoy never got around to using. It wouldn't have been too difficult to pick up, say, a hubcap or one of the scores of lunchroom trays that were lying around, take it away and claim that you had an 'original' piece of Purifoy, although perhaps it would be more like having an unopened tube of paint that had once belonged to Picasso. Actually it seemed far more likely that people might actually dump stuff there and create, as it were, new potential Purifoys, adding to the stack of materials rather than subtracting from it.

I was there on a Saturday afternoon, which I knew wasn't the best time. If I'd gone on a Monday morning I'm pretty sure I'd have had the whole place to myself. As it was, I'd been there maybe fifteen minutes when two cars arrived. Of course I could hardly object to the presence of other visitors, and you might think that ten acres would be enough room to absorb any number of art lovers. Not this lot however. Eight of them tumbled out of the cars, loud, exuberant, dumb, not as young as they were acting, somewhere between hipsters and assholes. Well, what else would you expect in a cool, desert sculpture park? But these idiots wanted to *give of themselves*: they wanted to be *creative*. They wanted to *make art*, and so they began playing with Noah Purifoy's stuff, moving things around, re-arranging them. I don't know that they were ruining it, but they were certainly messing with it. They were arrogant, stupid and presumptuous. I was cranking myself up to the point where I would have to do something, while also wondering whether telling them off might make things worse rather than better, when an old lady and her dog emerged from the trailer on the site; she'd obviously been in there all along, and she demanded to know what the hell this bunch thought they were doing.

'Oh, we're making our own sculptures,' one of them said.

The old lady told them in no uncertain terms that Noah Purifoy was an important artist with an international reputation, and they were not, and so they should keep their damn hands off things and have a little respect. It did the trick. It quieted them down a lot, and before long they left. I felt like a wimp, naturally, but I did have an excuse to exchange a few words with the old lady about how the young people of today had no sense of boundaries, and so on. She was the one who told me they were thinking of putting a fence around the place.

'So,' I said, 'do you live here?'

'No, I don't live here.'

'Did you know Noah Purifoy?'

'Yes, I knew Noah.'

Other attempts at conversation fell equally flat, and I didn't dare ask her the question that was uppermost in my mind. I knew that Noah Purifoy had died in pretty grim circumstances. The newspaper reports said he'd died in a fire in his home, and had been found by his caretaker, on the floor next to his wheelchair. I wanted to know whether that trailer the old lady had emerged from was the home in which Purifoy died, and whether she was the caretaker who'd found him. But I didn't ask. I didn't want her to think I was arrogant, stupid and presumptuous. I wanted her to know I had a sense of boundaries. We desert rats appreciate that in each other.

* * *

Am I a desert rat? Well, some days, yes, I like to think I am. There are times when I think the best, and on occasion the only, reason for living in Los Angeles is that you can get in your car and two hours later be walking in the Mojave Desert, one of the most rough and beautiful landscapes on earth. Deserts are not by any means always ruined places, though sometimes they are, the result of land degradation and poor farming methods. In the Mojave people are generally more concerned about the desert being ruined by off roaders, commercial interests and above all urban sprawl. Of course I don't want to see the Mojave damaged or destroyed, but I no longer fret about it quite the way I used to.

The fact is, when I made my first visits to the American desert and fell immediately in love, I was a bit of a prig. Unless the landscape was absolutely pristine, clean and utterly devoid of human presence (well, any human presence except mine, naturally) then I thought I was being cheated, being deprived of some big, deep, primal experience. I wanted something intense and cosmic and sublime. Well, I got over that. These days I look for human presence rather than absence, and specifically I look for the places where human concerns interact and intersect with the complete indifference of the desert. That this often involves ruin is a large part of the attraction.

It's always similar, but it's never the same twice. I'll be driving on a desert road, usually in California, usually in the Mojave, though it could be slightly farther away from home, a different desert, in Arizona or Nevada, and I'll see a ruined structure somewhere in the distance. I'll pull off the road, get out of the car, and start walking towards the ruin.

There's a specific kind of vernacular ruin you find in the American desert. The range is broad but hardly infinite. There are houses and shacks, of course, the odd farm or barn. Former motels, gas stations and restaurants are common, as are the remains of mining and chemical operations, along with the occasional abandoned drive-in theatre or airstrip.

I've explored a ruined health resort in the improbably named, and scarcely pronounceable, Zzyzx, once known as the Mineral Springs and Health Spa, run by a quack name of Curtis Howe Springer, who had an operation there from the forties to the seventies, before the Feds shut him down. The place still has the remains of a bungalow court where Springer's visitors stayed, along with some carefully planted, though now wayward, palm trees used to soften the desert view, and off to one side are the empty concrete baths where health seekers once soaked themselves. The baths are now bone dry, the paint and the very fabric of their walls is crumbling, and yet the location – empty pools, ruins, bare desert beyond – not only has a gorgeous, rugged, picturesque beauty, it also allows you to pretend you're in a J. G. Ballard story, probably 'The Voices of Time'.

> Later Powers often thought of Whitby, and the strange grooves the biologist had cut, apparently at random, all over the floor of the empty swimming pool. An inch deep and twenty feet long, interlocking to form an elaborate ideogram like a Chinese character, they had taken him all summer to complete, and he had obviously thought about little else, working away tirelessly through the long desert afternoons.

The Zzyzx site is now designated the Desert Studies Center, belonging to California State University, which has taken over some of the Springer buildings, though others have been left to decay; you might be surprised just how invasive untended palm trees can be. And behind one row of palms and some scrubby desert greenery, there's a showroom's worth of old, wrecked cars, dating from the early 1900s to the 1980s I'd guess, arranged side by side in a long, orderly row, rusting slowly, returning to the earth. I've walked around Zzyzx maybe ten times in the last twenty years and have seen exactly one other person there. We did not exchange greetings.

On the outskirts of Hinckley, the real-life location with the poisoned groundwater that features in the movie *Erin Brockovich*, and a town which seems frankly to be entirely made up of outskirts, I found what I eventually decided, and not with absolute confidence, was some kind of clandestine horticultural facility. It didn't look like that at first sight, and I'm pretty sure it started life as something else. There were two abandoned buildings, one a substantial, ranch-style bungalow made of rough though not local stone, and behind that a building about the size of a three-car garage, open to the elements on one side. Someone had painted KEEK OUT on one of the walls, but I did not keek out.

The bungalow was without doors, windows or ceilings, though it still had a roof, and the remains of what looked like a large professional-looking kitchen, though surely nobody would ever have run a restaurant out here. Only when I started poking around outside did things start to make some kind of sense. In what might have been the garden there was a set of metal struts and wires holding up some sheets of tattered black fabric: this I think was whatever the desert equivalent is of a cold frame, protecting plants from high rather than low temperatures. And in the open-sided garage building I found clusters of empty plant pots, many dozens of them, a box full of unused balls of string, then stacked outside in the rear, there were literally hundreds of empty plastic sacks that had once contained soil. And I found a boxed, unused, battery-operated soil-analysis kit that looked like a Geiger counter, complete with fresh sachets of cleaning and buffer solutions. I still have it and I really do intend to test my own soil with it one of these days.

I can't say I actually know with any certainty what went on in this place. It seemed the least likely site on which to try growing anything whatsoever: heat, sun, bad soil, no water, and no sign of an irrigation system as far as I could see. So you had to assume that whatever was being grown here was something that would justify and reward all that effort. Marijuana seemed a possibility, but it's hard to believe anyone ever thought they could make a go of it in this environment, and the evidence, of course, was that they hadn't. Maybe they should have tried growing cacti. And for all I know they did, and failed at that too. Some desert

ruins don't give up their stories however much you run the evidence through your imagination.

There are some structures on a hillside a little way outside Pioneertown (a place built as a semi-permanent set for cowboy movies, now a little Bohemian community) that from a distance look like log cabins, but the 'logs' are arranged vertically and made out of reinforced concrete, and it seems perfectly possible that they might have been something military: shelters or bunkers, or a gun range or places to test ordnance; or possibly they might have been needlessly elaborate animal pens, or just conceivably they might even have been homes.

And it is, inevitably, the ruined desert houses that are the most poignant, and in many ways the most mysterious. Imagining what it would be like to live out here, trying to make a life for yourself in this utterly inhospitable place, requires a good deal more empathy and imaginative energy that it does to imagine what it would have been like to, say, have lunch in a now ruined diner, or fill up at a now ruined gas station.

These ruined desert houses are also diverse to some extent, and often quite singular: I've wandered inside a big, abandoned, wooden teepee, stepped into a flimsy, half-built geodesic dome, explored something that looked like a watchtower; but many are very simple, no more than shacks, scarcely more than sheds, often with an air of improvisation, of amateurish construction skills, about them.

You assume the people must have been living pretty rough lives out here even at the best of times, baking under tin roofs, using, if they were lucky, a swamp cooler, trucking in their own water, relying on a portable generator. But at some point it all got too much for them; they moved on, they left a ruin behind, or perhaps it had turned into a ruin around them even while they lived there. They may have left in a hurry, or they may simply have been sloppy, or made indifferent by defeat, but there's a category of object that always gets left behind, lying around outside these ruined houses: car tyres, some outdated electrical appliances, quantities of not quite usable building materials. It's easy enough to see why they left that stuff behind. But some more personal, more domestic, things always get left behind too. There are always one or two children's toys, a grubby plastic doll with sand in her bodily cavities, a model car without wheels, a brightly coloured water pistol that's been stamped on. There are absolutely always shoes, and they always come singly: there will be a single sneaker alongside a single workboot, or perhaps a clear plastic mule alongside a black suede high heel, but there's never, ever, a matching pair. Do the people get to wherever they're going, find the other shoe, and then kick themselves and say, 'Oh damn, I left a perfectly good slingback out there in the sand'? Maybe.

There's always reading material in the ruins: books, generally something useful, rarely fiction or anything designed to entertain; more likely a truck-repair manual, a handbook on solar power, a guide to the night sky. My best find was a book to teach yourself Farsi, lightly annotated in spidery pencil.

Sometimes there's food left behind, an open pack of dry noodles, a bulging can of government potatoes, some 'butter+-flavor' Crisco. And inevitably, occasionally, there's the completely inexplicable: a Christmas tree complete with ornaments, a margarita glass in the shape of a cactus, a surfboard perforated with bullet holes.

* * *

Once in while there are enough ruined houses clustered together to constitute a ghost town. There may be a small question of definition here. How many ruins constitute a town? What are the elements of ghostliness? I once tracked down a ghost town I'd seen marked on a map and all I could find were a few concrete drainage pipes and an old computer monitor. It seemed neither a town, nor ghostly. In Death Valley I walked around in Skidoo, a town that thrived briefly in the first couple of decades of the twentieth century as the result of a gold find. There are no buildings there any more, hardly any sign of a town, but the hills are scattered with mining debris and a few open shafts, their entrances fenced (but I'm sure you could fall in if you were really determined). Ghostly? Well, it was a place where 'legend has it' the same man was hanged twice. A man named Hootch Simpson was foiled attempting to rob a bank, then killed the owner of the store where the bank was situated. The people of the town duly lynched Mr Simpson, and the next morning they lynched him again for the benefit of a press photographer who had by then arrived on the scene.

My favourite ghost town is Ballarat, just outside Death Valley. Here you can walk around a few ruined houses, some wood, some adobe; there's a jail, a graveyard, a mass of wrecked and ruined vehicles. Surprisingly, there's also a little museum-cum-store, run by a man named Rocky Novack, one of the town's few full-time inhabitants. Last time I was there he told me that Ballarat at that moment had a population of eight, mostly miners who lived in trailers and worked at the Briggs Mine a few miles down the road. It's a dirt road, of course.

There was an old pick-up truck displayed on a mound a short way from the store, an old Dodge Power Wagon. Novack assured me that this truck had once belonged to Charles Manson. I could see why he might say that. Once you're walking in Ballarat you're most definitely walking in Charles Manson's footsteps. The Manson Family used Ballarat as a gathering point before going deeper into the desert, to the Barker Ranch where they lived for a time. Even so, I was sceptical about the ownership of the truck. I'm no Manson obsessive but I'd read enough to know that Manson and his crew mostly used dune buggies and the occasional school bus for transport. However, it turns out there is some circumstantial evidence that the truck might have been Manson's. A book titled *Desert Shadows* by Bob Murphy, an eccentric but well-informed account of Manson in the desert, mentions the use of a few Dodge Power Wagons. One thing that makes me want to believe: the inside of the cab roof of this one is painted black with white stars, which certainly feels very period, and exactly the kind of thing one of those arty Manson girls might do. Novack says that people are always telling him he should put it up for sale on eBay, but he can see the inevitable problems of establishing provenance, to say nothing of the problems of shipping it to the successful bidder.

* * *

There are certain places in the desert that are constantly teetering on the brink, but never quite give up the ghost. Amboy, about two hundred miles east of Los Angeles, is one of these. It definitely was a town once, but right now there are SUVs driving down the freeway with larger populations than Amboy, and the freeway is precisely the reason for Amboy's demise.

It sits along a stretch of Route 66, the Mother Road, the place allegedly, formerly, to get your kicks, and when, in the 1950s, the Interstate 40 was built, some ten miles to the north, the serious cross-country traffic went there, leaving Amboy behind, to fade and desiccate, and remain a rough time capsule. But if I hesitate to call Amboy a town, I hesitate even more to call it a ghost town. The place has certainly been abandoned and neglected. Parts of it have certainly decayed and crumbled, and parts of it do indeed lie in ruin, but not all of it, and not all of it conspicuously. The most important parts, the most eye-catching, don't look like ruins at all, at least not at first glance.

What's there looks, from a distance, remarkably well-preserved. There's a school, a gas station, a church, a motel, a graveyard, a post office; the last of these is fully functional, but a close look reveals considerable ruin elsewhere. That church, for instance, which is actually a bare meeting hall, has a wooden tower with a cross on top, but although the walls are bright white and appear recently painted, the tower is leaning precariously, a little more every time I visit, and I don't doubt that one day I'll arrive there and find that gravity has completed its work. Part of the motel consists of a long row of neat, minimalist white cabins that look intact, and even habitable. But they're not. A closer look reveals that these cabins, which you can walk right into, are empty, with no furniture, no plumbing, no power, with the tatters of old linoleum on the floor, many windows smashed and broken Route 66 Cola bottles strewn around.

The gas station probably can't be considered a ruin at the moment, since it currently has gas for sale, though there were many years when it didn't. There was a period when dangerous-looking yet surprisingly friendly bikers would hang out there on Sunday afternoons, selling only slightly overpriced beer from an ice-filled cooler. They did a reasonable trade, I think. Plenty of people stop in Amboy: it's hard not to. Right between the gas station and the motel is one of the greatest stop-you-in-your-tracks roadside advertising signs any of us is ever likely to see.

The sign says Roy's Motel Café, and it's a classic all right: tall, formidable, red, black and blue, two rectangles and a downward-pointing arrowhead, a smack-you-in-the-eye typeface, and, more to the point, right in the middle it says VACANCY. Many a photographer (not least William Egglestone, who photographed it back in the day when there was often a classic black-and-white police cruiser parked outside) has embraced that visual and verbal pun: the presence of gas, food and lodging here, nothing but absence down the road. Is that a bit too obvious, a bit too much of a cliché? You bet. And so the sign has appeared in multiple movies, music videos, TV commercials and photo shoots.

This is the secret of Amboy's 'success'. Although it has defining elements of ruin, it has other elements that define it as a stage or movie set, as a moody, evocative backdrop, as a location. This inevitably creates certain problems for people (such as me) who yearn for an (admittedly contested) authenticity when they're walking in the desert and in ruins.

In fact there's at least one place near by where people do some more or less conventional, and fairly strenuous, desert hiking. The Amboy Crater is just a few miles to the west, an extinct cinder-cone volcano, two hundred and fifty feet high, surrounded by a black lava field. It's popular to the extent that I've even seen tour buses unloading some extraordinarily well-dressed sightseers there, though I didn't stick around to see how far they walked.

But let's face it, an extinct volcano in the middle of the desert barely fits within even the broadest notion of ruin. If you're looking for ruin, you have to look elsewhere, and as it happens Route 66 is not the only transport artery to pass through Amboy. There's a railway line too, running parallel to the road, a couple of hundred yards to the south, and the railroad is still very much in business. If you hang out in Amboy for an hour or so, chances are you'll see a couple of immensely long freight trains roll through, with the initials BNSF on the locomotives, standing for Burlington Northern Sante Fe.

I do like railways. I like to watch the trains go by. I like to stare down the tracks towards the vanishing point. Doesn't everybody? And yet cities, buildings, landscapes, even small desert towns, so often turn their back on the railway. Trains thread through the bad parts of town, behind high walls and fences, in cuttings and tunnels, present but not seen and not regarded. Meanwhile the land beside the tracks becomes a no man's land where debris collects, where things get dumped, where graffiti are largely tolerated because at least they're not somewhere more conspicuous. In the desert, however, the railways have nowhere to hide.

And whereas in England every yard of track is fenced off in an attempt to make it inaccessible and supposedly safe, here in the wide open spaces of the desert nobody has the time, energy or money to fence off all those thousands of miles. A man can walk right up to the tracks, walk across them, along them if he wants to. Oh sure, there'll be the occasional No Trespassing sign, but who's going to take any notice? Who's going to police it? And of course dumping goes on there with a casual lack of inhibition. Down by the tracks in Amboy there used to be a sign that said No Dumping, standing guard over a great heap of dumped garbage.

And let's face it, the railway people themselves are a messy bunch. In Amboy there's a sprawling three-sided corral where they've stored, or at least stashed, various bits of miscellaneous railroad hardware: posts, coils, wiring, chunks of lumber – and those glass-and-porcelain electrical connectors, though those tend to be smashed if they're not stolen. You can walk into the corral, pick around, and although there isn't a sign saying 'Help Yourself', equally there's no sign saying 'Keep Out', and you can't help thinking that if you had a use for some scrap fence posts or wiring, the guys from the BNSF would understand, and definitely wouldn't put much effort into stopping you.

As I turned my back on the preserved charm of Roy's Motel Café and Route 66, I was aware that maybe I wasn't so much walking in ruins as strolling around in mess, performing the pedestrian equivalent of making mud pies, as I admired stacks of old sleepers and heaps of ballast. I don't think there's anything wrong with that, but sometimes it's good to aim a little higher, so when I noticed a fine, low-slung industrial building maybe a third of a mile away along the tracks, I decided to walk over and look around. I would have accepted that this wasn't ruin exploration on the very grandest scale, but we all have to do what we can.

From the road, when I set off walking, I couldn't have said what the building was intended for; something to do with the railway obviously, perhaps loading and unloading, possibly connected with storage, though there was no indication that anything was going on there at the moment. At first I thought it was made of white painted metal and the paint had rusted or flaked off, but as I got a little closer I realised the walls were broad slabs of wood and the paint had peeled away in long vertical strips giving the effect of corrugations. Up against the side of the building I could see storage tanks, some wooden pallets, a mobile scaffolding tower, and there was a chain-link fence around the whole thing, serious but hardly impenetrable. There didn't seem to be much in there that anyone would want to steal. I guessed they were trying to keep out vandals and graffiti sprayers, but since I was neither of the above I eyed the fence and wondered if I should do a little creative trespass – in other words, shimmy over and go inside.

I walked a circuit of the perimeter. A railway siding ran alongside the back of the building within the fence, and there was no sign of life or activity anywhere. Some big roller doors on the building were raised and you could see there was nothing at all inside. I got the impression that if this place was still being used for anything, it wasn't much and it wasn't recent. I decided I'd go in.

And then, as I was reaching for a handhold on the chain-link, I realised the place wasn't deserted after all. Around the side next to some half-demolished walls that looked like they might have belonged to a coal bunker, there was a single, very clean, shiny, dinky little golf cart with a canopy, a thing wildly out of place in this battered, industrial-desert scene, and sitting in the cart was a huge man, dressed all in white. As I remember it he was wearing a solar topi, though I think I may have made that up in retrospect; it may just have been a floppy sunhat, but nevertheless the overall effect was undoubtedly grand, spooky and strangely ethereal. He looked both ghostly and angelic, unworldly, very,

very still, not remotely right for this location. He was also wearing wrap-around shades, and he was smoking a long thin cigar, and he reminded me of Marlon Brando, certainly not as he was in *The Wild One*, and only partly as he was in *Apocalypse Now*, but rather as he appeared in *The Island of Dr Moreau*, where he dresses in white gauze, presumably to hide his bulk, with his face coated in white pancake for reasons known only to himself. I'm prepared to believe that time and my imagination may have glorified the stature and strangeness of my man in Amboy, but not by much. His presence seemed genuinely uncanny and alarming. A man who can invoke Marlon Brando, a ghost and an angel, while sitting in a golf cart obviously has an undeniable aura.

I think he must have seen me before I saw him, and the sunglasses ensured there was nothing so unsubtle as eye-contact, but he turned his head just a fraction in my direction, then back again, the subtlest admonitory shake of the head, as if to say, 'I wouldn't do that if I were you. I wouldn't do that if you know what's good for you.'

I like to think I know what's good for me. I stepped away from the fence, calmly, unhurriedly, walked on, went about my business, and eventually I headed back to the car, parked up by Roy's sign. My wife was waiting for me there; she'd been off in the other direction, looking at the school, and she asked me what I'd been doing.

'Oh,' I said, 'I think I saw the god of the ruins of Amboy.'

'Was he on a train?'

'No.'

'Was he walking?'

'He was on a golf cart.'

'Makes sense. What's that in your hand?'

What I had in my hand was one of my great desert finds. Not so long ago it was thought of as perfectly OK to collect rocks or fossils or antlers or even plant specimens from the desert; now this is regarded as environmentally unsound, as messing with nature, as pure evil. So now I only pick up stuff that doesn't belong there, that's been left or dumped by humans: antique car parts are a particular favourite, and the best stuff is up on my garage wall. What I'd picked up that day, after my encounter by the chain-link fence, was half of one of those diamond-shaped metal signs that they put on the back of vehicles, in this case railway trucks, warning of dangerous cargoes. This one would have read Spontaneous Combustion, but since I only had the left-hand half, it read Sponta Combu, a great name for something – a band, a spy, a guru, an Indian fusion dish – or maybe it's one of the ninety-nine names of the god of the ruins of Amboy.

* * *

My wife and I were in Nevada when we saw a couple of wrecked buildings adjacent to each other on the same plot of land. One was a house with smashed windows and walls, and a fallen tree resting against its roof. The other was a long, low structure, rustic in a way, and we wondered if it might have been a farm building, maybe a battery house for chickens. The prospect of walking around a defunct factory farm was both horrifying and irresistible. We ignored the sign painted on a giant water tank by the gate that said 'Closed. Beat It!' and we walked inside the grounds, heading for the long low building.

Well before we got to it, we could tell this was no factory farm. We could see carpet and fake wood panelling inside. The building had evidently been inhabited by humans, but as we climbed up some sagging wooden steps that led inside we were still puzzled about what kind of place this was. We stepped into a broad central corridor with many rooms leading off on either side. Was it a motel? Well, it certainly didn't feel like it; the rooms were far too small to be motel rooms, and most of them didn't have bathrooms. And then we noticed the ceiling, which was sprayed with some kind of glittering popcorn texture. And looking around we saw that in certain areas there was carpet on the walls as well as on the floor, all the way up to the ceiling, chunky thick shag, and some of the doors were a shocking pink colour, and in one spot there was a big hole in the floor where a hot tub had been.

Although there were beds in some of the rooms, they didn't look like real beds. They were circular or semicircular and some of them were far too small to sleep on, more like platforms on which a woman might dance semi-naked for the titillation of some paying customer. Yes, we were in a ruined brothel. The sign outside saying 'Beat it!' suddenly took on a new meaning.

I'm enough of a Reichian to entertain the idea that some orgone energy, created by concentrations of sexual activity, might still have been lurking around the place, but there was no feeling of that here. And if there had ever been the detritus of commercial sex – porn, stripper shoes or sex toys – they had been taken away by souvenir hunters. One room did in fact have a video recorder, but it was a Betamax. Outside, strewn across the ground, there was a layer of ancient, smashed TVs and computers, which might well have been used for X-rated entertainment, but the only video tape we could find was *Beverly Hills Cop II.*

Between the main house and what we were now calling (in heavily flagged inverted commas) 'the chicken house' we did find a kind of bunker, amazingly solid, unnecessarily so you'd have thought, made of cinder blocks, with a deep, dark basement. I eased myself down the half-dozen dirt and concrete stairs and stared into the gloom. If this had been a movie there would surely have been chains, dubious fluids staining the walls, a torn item or two of lingerie, but this basement was a giant, free-range rodent nest. I scuttled back up, all too aware of the risks of hantavirus.

* * *

The next day we were chewing the fat with the owner of a roadside junk-and-rock store, a God-fearing man (he gave us some pamphlets), friendly, chatty, sunburned, snaggle-toothed, with a very conspicuous basal cell carcinoma (aka a rodent ulcer) on his cheek. Without us bringing up the subject, he told us that things were bad all over for the Nevada brothel trade. The brothels relied on truckers for their business, he said, and as the price of gas had gone up, drivers' margins had been cut to the bone. Frittering away money on some roadside relief would have wiped out the profit completely. This surprised me a little. I don't doubt that truckers are very good at calculating profit and loss, but who knew they had such impulse control?

A couple of days after that we were on the outskirts of Beatty, a three-casino town with a chemical and radioactive-waste dump on the outskirts, and saw, with amazement, and a kind of glee, a wrecked aeroplane lying right by the side of the road. It was small, a six-seater at most. It seemed unlikely that the plane had crashed precisely where it was, though it would have been even more surprising if somebody had gone to the trouble of moving it there.

We investigated the plane and we saw it was a complete mess, with broken windows, engines missing and the tail thoroughly smashed, while the interior of the cockpit was destroyed in a way that wouldn't have been accounted for simply by a crash. Nor would a crash have explained all the rock-band stickers on the fuselage, and it definitely didn't explain the one that read: 'I Got an STD, R 2010.' But ultimately that was the most comprehensible of all. I'd been too fascinated by the plane to notice the surrounding territory. The nose was pointing in the direction of a tall yellow and black sign some twenty or thirty yards away. The sign read, in full: 'Brothel, Angel's Ladies, Free All Night Truck Parking, Free Showers, Free Coffee, Phones, Massages, Open 24/7, 365 days.' The sign didn't lie. This brothel was alive and well and open for business. And if you might argue that having a wrecked plane as a roadside attraction to draw folks to your business was a little over-freighted with the symbolism of ruin, there was no denying its effectiveness.

Not only was Angel's Ladies in business then, it still is at the time of writing; they even have a website, simple, a little messy, but informative enough. It tells you for instance that the plane has been there since the brothel's grand opening day in 1978, when the owner placed a mattress on the ground in the parking lot, and offered a freebie to any parachutist who could hit the mark. Quite a few were willing to try, jumping from a small plane brought in specially for the purpose. The plane went up, the day was blustery, the girls stood on the ground waving up at the punters, and it seems that the pilot must have been distracted by all this hoopla. He circled the area, hit a cross wind, clipped a high wire, plunged out of the sky, and crash-landed in the dirt. The people in the plane were fine, but the plane itself was a wreck, and it has stayed more or less where it landed ever since.

The website's menu invites you to click on a section for employment opportunities. As part of the benefits they say:

> You can enjoy our facilities which include –
> A 65,000 gallon hot mineral swimming pool.
> A hot tub filled with tantalising mineral water.
> Enjoy walking and hiking on our 80 acre ranch.
> No other brothel offers these kind of facilities.
> Must be 21 years old.

Now, I've never claimed to know much about what the harlots of Nevada demand in their working conditions, but I'd have thought that 'walking and hiking' opportunities would have been pretty low on the list of priorities. I'm delighted to have been proved wrong. The idea that working girls like to stroll through the desert, occasionally poking around in the ruins, pleases me no end.

6

Walking in Prison, and in the Future with Samuel Beckett and Others

POZZO: I am blind.
(Silence.)
ESTRAGON: Perhaps he can see into the future.

Samuel Beckett, *Waiting for Godot*

In these regions we find hardly a mile without a ruin . . . and, in places, mile after mile and square mile upon square mile of ruin. It is a luxuriance of ruin; and there is not a large ruin in the country which does not prove upon examination to be the composition of ruins more ancient still.

Sir Richard Francis Burton, *Unexplored Syria*

Enormous prison, like a hundred thousand cathedrals, never anything else any more, from this time forth, and in it, somewhere, perhaps, riveted, tiny, the prisoner . . .

Samuel Beckett, *The Unnamable*

They went on in the perfect blackness, sightless as the blind. Nights dark beyond darkness and the days more grey each one than what had gone before. Smell of earth and wet ash in the rain. Dark water in the roadside ditch. We were always lucky. You'll be lucky again. How long have you been on the road? I was always on the road.

I could go on, but I won't go on. This is my own cut-up, or collage, or possibly mash-up, of sentences taken from *The Road*, Cormac McCarthy's 2006 novel, set in a post-apocalyptic world, in which an unnamed father and son walk across a ruined America. I wouldn't be so foolish as to suggest that I've 'improved' McCarthy's text, but I think I've made it read a lot more like Samuel Beckett. I have my reasons for doing this, which will become apparent.

The America depicted in *The Road* is cold, devoid of colour, the daylight is ashen, and the boy has an irritating habit of addressing his father as 'Papa'. They are not the only two people left in the world, but the few other survivors are not be trusted, they're 'bad guys', homicidal, and in some cases cannibalistic. At least one of them resembles a tramp out of Samuel Beckett, 'shuffling along the road before them, dragging one leg slightly and stopping from time to time to stand stooped and uncertain before setting out again'.

Eventually father and son come upon the ruins of a 'once grand house . . . a fireplace with raw brick showing where the wooden mantel and surround had been pried away and burned . . . trash piled everywhere . . . smell of rust and excrement'.

Set in the floor of one of the rooms of the house is a padlocked hatch. The father smashes it open and takes a few steps down into the basement where he sees that 'huddled against the back wall were naked people, male and female, all trying to hide, shielding their faces with their hands. On the mattress lay a man with his legs gone to the hip and the stumps of them blackened and burnt.' The people are being imprisoned by 'four bearded men and two women', and although the book isn't absolutely explicit, the implication is that these prisoners are there as livestock. The passage is likely to make the reader think of concentration camps, torture chambers, the ruined prisons of Piranesi, as well as the abattoir, and perhaps also Plato's *Republic*, Book VII, which describes prisoners in an underground den, where they've been since childhood, chained in a way that guarantees they can't escape and can't even turn their heads. Some way above and behind them is a blazing fire, and a low wall, along which men walk carrying vessels, statues and figures of animals. The prisoners only see the shadows projected from behind them. They mistake the shadow world for the real world, and by Plato's logic we have a philosophical and moral duty to release some of the prisoners and let them walk into the light and see the real world, even if it blinds them at first. Their job is then to return in order to free and enlighten the other prisoners; a jailbreak in the name of philosophical truth.

The fact that Cormac McCarthy's hero fails to free the prisoners in the basement of the ruined house, in fact turns down their pleas for help, makes him morally ambiguous, but a survivor. He's in business to save his son, who is referred to towards the end of the book not as the light but as the fire. 'It's inside you. It was always there. I can see it.' Depending on your prejudices you will either find this spiritually uplifting or mawkish claptrap. I'm pretty sure I know which side Samuel Beckett would have been on.

* * *

Nobody doubts that the future, like L. P. Hartley's past, will be another country, and that they will do things *very* differently there, not least walking. One now outdated, prophetic vision of the future, imagined a society where walking, and possibly even legs, had become obsolete, thanks to moving pavements, personal hovercraft, one-person helicopters and so on, or even telekinesis. In this scenario, pedestrianism would at best be a thing of the past, at worst, as in Ray Bradbury's short story 'The Pedestrian', a legally forbidden activity. Of course you might think that even in the future the best way to promote pedestrianism (or anything else) might actually be to forbid it, though this obviously doesn't apply to Bradbury's fictional Los Angeles of 2025.

Today's 'futurologists' are more likely to be in favour of forbidding heavy technology, above all the internal combustion engine, and they tend to reimagine the city as a decentred place of walker-friendly streets, neighbourhoods and, of course, *communities*. Some even see this as a return to a kinder, gentler, golden age of pedestrianism, although those who have read about, say, the chamber-pot-emptying habits of medieval Edinburgh housewives – a shout of 'Gardy-loo!' to warn those walking in the street below, and then the deluge – or have read statistics about how much horse manure was dumped on the streets of New York City in the early 1890s – five hundred tons per day – may wonder precisely where and when this pedestrian paradise was actually located. We might even wonder if the arrival of the motor car didn't actually make streets cleaner and pleasanter for walkers.

Certain science-fiction movies have regularly envisaged a time in the future when walking is the only viable means of getting around, either because the oil has simply run out, or (more cinematically) has fallen into the hands of psychopathic warlords, so that there will still be a few cool vehicles thrashing through the wasteland, even as most survivors are condemned to plod along on foot. George Miller's *Mad Max* (1979) created the mould here and it's scarcely been broken since.

Mad Max's walking style – tattered leather motorcycle suit, big gun in one hand and a dog at his side – scarcely seems improvable, and has certainly not been improved on. Arnold Schwarzenegger's Terminator, seen in four movies to date, tweaks the image just a little: a bigger gun, sometimes two, the addition of sunglasses, but the absence of a dog. Add yes, the warriors of the wasteland may sometimes be female and not always in leather – think Milla Jovovich in *Resident Evil: Extinction* (2007), where she wears fabric rather than a leather suit, thereby allowing her to show her stocking tops – but the basic design elements for distressed, post-apocalyptic pedestrian chic remain pretty much unchanged.

You might think that a woman walking through the wasteland with her stocking tops on display would have more rather than less use for a faithful hound, but Alice, Jovovich's character, gets by without one. Compare and contrast with the 1975 movie *A Boy and His Dog*, based on stories by Harlan Ellison in which Vic (the boy played by Don Johnson) and Blood (his dog) walk through the California desert, communicating telepathically. There were in fact those, including Harlan Ellison himself, who reckon that Cormac McCarthy's *The Road* borrowed a little too heavily from that work. I don't make any huge claims for these movies, and I admit that I watched them all chiefly because I was seduced by movie stills that showed people walking in ruins.

I'm more inclined to make claims for the movie *The Book of Eli* (2010), in which the eponymous hero, played by Denzel Washington, doesn't have a dog, largely I suspect because the creators feared it would give too much away. The movie is set, as ever, in a ruined future, this time after the 'the war tore a hole in the sky'. Consequently everybody has to wear sunglasses when they walk outside, to protect them from the devastating sun, and Eli wears them too, because it would again give too much away if he didn't.

Eli has been walking west across America for thirty years, and when somebody asks, 'How do you know you're walking the right way?' he replies, 'Faith.' He is certainly not relying on visual clues. Very late in the movie, in what you may consider either a brilliant twist or a simple cheat, we discover that Eli is in fact blind, so presumably he doesn't actually need the shades, though he could surely use a faithful hound. Blindness certainly doesn't inhibit his fighting skills with guns and swords, though it may explain why it's taken him such a long time to walk across the country.

He does finally make it to the west, not solely by walking but also travelling by truck and rowing boat. And the particular bit of the west he arrives at is Alcatraz, San Francisco's infamous island prison, still heavily guarded in this cinematic future, but turned into a kind of rebuilt American Alexandrian Library. Inside it Lombardi, the kindly, white-haired curator, played by

Malcolm McDowell, gathers in the surviving cultural fragments of the destroyed world. They have Shakespeare and most of the volumes of the *Encyclopaedia Britannica*, but no Bible.

Happily, Eli has memorised the entire King James Bible and duly recites it, in its entirety it would appear, as the curator obligingly writes it all down in long hand. Biblical concordances show that this task would involve saying, and therefore writing, the word 'walk', along with its attendant forms (walking, walkest, walketh), literally hundreds of times, including walking in the Valley of the Shadow of Death, in the gardens of Eden and Gethsemane and, of course, in the ways of the Lord.

The word 'ruin', in any form, occurs far less often, which surprised me. I had a notion that the Bible was in some ways a handbook of ruin, especially the Old Testament; it's a big volume, and humanity's ruination comes in the third chapter of the first book, but the word itself appears just a score of times. Certainly the Bible describes civilisations that fall into and rise from ruins, depending on the extent to which they do or don't please God, but I'd been expecting something rather zestier than,

> Thy riches, and thy fairs, thy merchandise, thy mariners, and thy pilots, thy calkers, and the occupiers of thy merchandise, and all thy men of war, that are in thee, and in all thy company which is in the midst of thee, shall fall into the midst of the seas in the day of thy ruin.

That's Ezekiel 27:27, and quite a tricky passage for Eli to have memorised, I should think.

Parts of *The Book of Eli* were filmed in the real Alcatraz: the long central corridor through which Malcolm McDowell walks with Denzel Washington in crucial scenes in the movie is quite recognisable as the central corridor of the Cellhouse, known colloquially as Broadway. I know because I've walked along it.

* * *

I think I wouldn't have done very well in Alcatraz. I'm sure I wouldn't do very well in any prison, but here I'd have had special problems. For one thing, new arrivals were forced to strip naked and walk through that central corridor, with three levels of caged prisoners on either side, the cells closing in as they got higher, daylight visible a long, long way above. The inmates would look out and down on their naked, newly arrived brethren, rattle the bars, yell and hoot, offering a derisive welcome that perhaps meant, 'One of us,' or possibly, 'Ah, fresh meat.'

After that first day, the opportunities for walking in or around Alcatraz would have been severely limited. The cells varied a little in size, but five feet by nine was typical, scarcely enough room to pace back and forth like a caged animal. True, there were short walks to be had, three times a day, to and from the dining hall, and perhaps the occasional longer walk to the warden's office, though that was surely a walk few inmates would want to take. Otherwise, on several days per week, the frequency depending on your status and trustworthiness as a prisoner, you'd be allowed into the recreation yard for exercise; if you misbehaved you'd be confined to your cell and not allowed to do any walking whatsoever.

I'll bet some of the prisoners didn't mind that so very much. The recreation yard, I can testify, is one of the bleakest, chilliest, least hospitable places in which one could ever set foot; the high-walled rectangle currently contains the remains of a baseball diamond, some scrubby grass and a flight of steps in one corner with risers so deep no human being could easily walk up them; the whole area is lashed by an icy marine wind that threatens to blow one off one's feet. I was not a prisoner, of course, not least because the prison shut down in 1963: I was merely one of the million and a half tourists who visit Alcatraz each year, to enjoy, among other attractions, an extensive self-guided walking tour.

There were precious few tourists in the recreation yard the

day I was there. It was mid-April and San Francisco itself was in the middle of an unexpectedly warm spell, but by the time the boat was halfway between the mainland and the landing dock on Alcatraz, the temperature had dropped scarily, and as we approached the island it was cloaked in cold, damp, spectral gloom.

I had taken the early boat to be ahead of the crowds but that meant I was not ahead of the coastal fog. My wife was with me, and she hadn't complained about the early rise, but she complained long and hard about the cold and damp. I hadn't even thought about the weather. I'd been more concerned with whether Alcatraz can really be considered a ruin. It certainly had some of the elements, but how ruined can a place be when a million and a half tourists pass through it every year? And as the boat docked, I looked at the various structures visible on the island, and OK, they looked careworn, the paint peeling, the colours washed out, but they also looked ominously solid. Directly adjacent to the dock, for instance, was Building 64, where the guards and their families used to live, a hefty brick and stone structure, with stylish verandahs and all its windows intact. Nearby was a guard tower, perfectly usable it seemed if you had anything to guard, with a surprisingly elegant spiral staircase running up through its core. Other buildings looked four-square and well-built, qualities you would certainly want in a prison, but qualities that threatened to disappoint the lover of ruins.

There were some graffiti, the clearest of which read 'Indians Welcome', but these were historic artifacts, dating from the occupation of Alcatraz in 1969 and 1970 when a group of American Indians, and then various San Francisco types, landed on the island to claim it as Native American territory. The graffiti are, of course, now being carefully preserved. In fact there was a fire during the occupation which destroyed various buildings, and surely added to the ruin, but I couldn't see any signs of this as yet.

And then I spotted something. High on the rock, right behind Building 64, and with a lighthouse rising through the mist beyond it, was something that looked like an honest-to-goodness ruin: a roofless, windowless confection, some of its walls missing, the whole thing crumbling at the edges like hard cheese. This, I knew, was the warden's house. I was enormously encouraged and relieved by its distressed state. I would be able to walk in ruins after all.

Fortunately, once I set foot on the island and began the ascent of the main path, steep enough for a tram to be provided for non-walkers (though the powers that be stress this is only for those with genuine disabilities, not for those who are simply idle), I realised that I needn't have fretted at all. There was ruin galore on all sides, and even some of the buildings that had looked solid from the boat proved satisfying porous when seen up close.

The Post Exchange and Officer Club, for example, was a ruin in the classic manner, an accumulation of square, concrete openings, arranged in receding planes, each one framing the opening behind. Tendrils of rebar were visible, there was moss coating the outer fringes and seagulls had colonised the inner-most reaches. Beyond that was a warehouse and a power plant, the latter perhaps not a genuine ruin since it was still generating electricity, but beside it were a couple of dumpsters stencilled with the words 'Alcatras [*sic*]: concrete debris only'. The process of ruin was evidently ongoing. A lone seagull stood sentry on the lid of the dumpster.

At the far end of the island were a couple of buildings that any admirer of functionalist Bauhaus architecture would cherish: the Modern Industries Building and the New Industries Building, a pair of unmatching but not dissimilar geometrical masses, the

former three storeys, the latter two storeys, each with as much window as wall, small-scale factories where the inmates had worked, gaining skills, manufacturing furniture, brushes, gloves and uniforms; attempts at rehabilitation that had only been intermittently successful.

The Modern Industries Building was securely fenced off, and the Dead End sign attached to the chain-link seemed a little superfluous to me. But the upper floor of the New Industries Building was perfectly accessible, a long, open, bare, clean space, once dedicated solely to laundry, with many regularly placed columns and internal walls made up of panes of wired glass. Most of the panes were discoloured a rusty brown, and many were broken, but the wire ensured that the glass fragments remained in place like fractured, crystalline spiderwebs. Light fixtures, pipes and chunks of mysterious hardware hung from the ceiling; this was a fine and beautifully austere place. You couldn't help thinking if it had been just about anywhere else it would not have been left in ruins, that some artful developer would have 'repurposed' it and turned it into highly desirable loft-style apartments. Maybe they will yet.

Elsewhere around the island, broken parapets and stairways, with their attendant signs saying 'Area Closed for Your Safety', suggested this wasn't an entirely neutered version of ruin, that there was some danger and risk if you were determined to find it. And at one end of the island, right at the water's edge, were features described in the guidebook as 'rubble piles', *disjecta* from the prison buildings, most too broken down to be easily identified, though there were a few more or less recognisable fragments of wall and balustrade sinking into the lush greenery that grew up around them, while cormorants preened near by.

I was by no means alone as I walked around and peered at the external decay of Alcatraz, and I did find myself wondering why quite so many do visit these particular ruins. Fame no doubt has something to do with it. People come to Alcatraz because it's famous: it's famous because so many people visit. And certainly there's brand-name recognition, and it's a catchy name, from A to Z, much mentioned and promoted on TV and in movies, in fiction and in the memoirs of both guards and inmates, the former home of Al Capone, 'Machine Gun' Kelly, Mickey Cohen. Quite a few murders were committed there, prisoners killing guards or each other. There were some impressive escapes. Some people will tell you that ghosts still walk there, though I think they're generally people who want to sell you something, such as a guidebook to the ghosts of Alcatraz.

But essentially, ghosts or not, I think people do go there to scare themselves a little, to have the thrill of imagining what it might have been like to be a prisoner here, locked up in what was historically America's toughest penitentiary, in company with the worst of the worst. Of course they're primarily trying to imagine how it *felt*, but in order to do that, they first have to imagine, or imaginatively reconstruct, the physical world of the prison in its unruined state. They have to be able to envisage the warden's house intact, the industry buildings with their windows unbroken, with sewing and washing machines in place. Naturally there were mechanisms to help with this, old photographs, information boards, and inside a museum-quality Perspex case there was a beautifully detailed architectural scale model showing Alcatraz as it had been in its prime. A lot of people were taking pictures of that.

Equally you had to unimagine some of the improvements. The gardens for instance, tended by teams of volunteers, were spectacular, with an agave trail around the eastern end of the island, though that was only 'seasonally open', perhaps because a casual stroller might disappear into the mist, slip on the ruins and be blown away into the ocean.

But chiefly this act of imagination was achieved by visiting the Cellhouse, the place where the prisoners were locked up behind bars, the place where the fresh intake of prisoners was forced to walk naked, where Malcolm McDowell had walked with Denzel Washington in the movie. The cells were only ruined to a limited degree. There had been a toilet in each cell, and these had either been removed or blocked up, but apart from that the cells were pretty much the way they'd been when the prison was in business. The cells were so simple, so stark, so primitive, that there really wasn't much that ruination could do to them.

As you entered the cellblock you were offered, in fact given whether you wanted it or not, a digital player, the delivery system for the audio tour. You strapped on the headset, pressed play, and various recorded voices, both prisoners and guards, told the story of the prison. This was perfectly good in one sense: informative, anecdotal, grimly entertaining. On the other hand it felt a mite repressive. The voices instructed you where to walk, where to stop, where to turn, where to look. Before very long I'd had enough of that and I slipped off the headset and simply walked wherever I felt like going. Of course, I missed some information, but it seemed a small price to pay for what felt like freedom. Foucault might have been proud of me. I'm not trying to make any great claims for myself as a subversive or rule-breaker – and we know those types did especially badly on Alcatraz – but I didn't actually see anybody else unshackling themselves from the audio tour and walking their own course.

We had come on an early boat, so there weren't many people on the rock when we arrived. But boats landed every half-hour or so, each one delivering about two hundred and fifty people, which is more or less the number of prisoners incarcerated in Alcatraz at any one time. Since it takes much longer than half an hour to walk round the place, in the early part of the day there were inevitably far more people arriving than departing, and I got the unsettling sense of being part of a burgeoning, overcrowded prison population, competing for space, air, resources.

The crowd inside the Cellhouse walked slowly. They looked lost, their faces vacant. They were paying attention to the voices in the headset, to voices in their head. Listening to the audio tour caused them to move slowly and deliberately, walking, standing, turning and looking as they were told to do. I can't say they looked precisely like zombies, since they didn't have that old zombie shamble, but then again they didn't look very alive either. They looked as though their walking was controlled by external forces, which in a sense it was. They floated, appeared ethereal, wraithlike, moving in a loose pattern, not absolutely in sync with each other since everybody's recorded commentary had started at a different moment, and yet the pace and rhythm was uniform and constant. They were much more measured than you'd expect a crowd in a prison to be. They were cut off from each other, not talking, not sharing any of the gallows humour that you might have expected.

It seemed like a moment to quote, or at least garble, perhaps mash up, some lines from T. S. Eliot's *The Waste Land*:

Unreal City,
Under the brown fog of a winter dawn . . .
I had not thought death had undone so many . . .
'Are you alive, or not? Is there nothing in your head?'

I thought I would share this with my wife, and I looked around for her, and she was nowhere to be seen. We'd gone our separate ways in the Cellhouse. I had found the prison library more fascinating than she had – rows of totally empty shelves, not a book in sight, no Shakespeare, no *Encyclopaedia*, no Bible – and she'd gone off to see the kitchen and dining-room, but we had had no doubt that we'd find each other again without much difficulty. Now I realised it was some time since I'd seen her and I did a swift circuit of the Cellblock, including a clothed walk down Broadway, but the prison now seemed labyrinthine and much more complex than it had appeared earlier, the crowd was larger than ever, and although I encountered many lost souls I couldn't find my wife. This went on much longer than I wanted it to.

It would be foolish to pretend that this really caused me any great existential dread. I did find her eventually, though in fact not very soon, in the gift shop looking at a shelf displaying lumps of concrete, pieces of Alcatraz 'Not available elsewhere', the concrete debris that I imagine had been contained in that 'Alcatras' dumpster with the seagull on top now being flogged to souvenir hunters. Even so, there had been something strangely unnerving and unsettling about searching through crowded prison corridors, looking for someone, and seeing only lost souls who were absorbed in their own private hell, or audio tours.

'What? Are you here?' I said when I found her.

'Are you really quoting T. S. Eliot at me?' she said with some disdain.

'You're right,' I said. 'I should probably be quoting Samuel Beckett.'

* * *

And which words of Samuel Beckett should I have been quoting? Well, my immediate thought, inspired by the mindless drift of the Alcatraz tourists and the oddly discomforting search for my spouse, was of *The Lost Ones*, a short prose piece that Beckett began in 1966 and completed in 1970. This isn't exactly a prison drama, though it has elements of one, being set in an 'abode where lost bodies roam each searching for its lost one'. Beckett's 'prison' is a flattened rubber cylinder, fifty metres in circumference and sixteen metres high, the light is dim, the temperature fluctuates wildly, and two hundred lost souls, who have one square metre of space each, walk around, not without purpose but largely without hope. As they walk, they brush against each other making the sound of dead leaves, but their feet make no sound on the rubber floor.

And if it's a major stretch to compare my temporary plight in Alcatraz with the plight of Beckett's lost souls, the fact is you don't have to read very far in Beckett to encounter lots of walking and ruin. There's Molloy, walking with one leg shorter than the other, there's the narrator of 'First Love' who walks happily in graveyards, 'I take the air there willingly.' Watt whose

> way of advancing due east, for example, was to turn his bust as far as possible towards the north and at the same time to fling out his right leg as far as possible towards the south, and

> then to turn his bust as far as possible towards the south and at the same time to fling out his left leg as far as possible towards the north, and then again to turn his bust as far as possible towards the north and to fling out his right leg as far as possible towards the south.

There's Bellacqua in *More Pricks Than Kicks*:

> 'I went out to walk it off.'
>
> 'Walk what off?' cried Lucy. She was sick and tried of his moods.
>
> 'Oh, I don't know,' he said, 'our old friend, the devil's bath.'

For years I thought the devil's bath was alcohol, and that Bellacqua was out walking off either drunkenness or a hangover, but eventually I realised the reference is actually to Robert Burton's *Anatomy of Melancholy*, in which the devil's bath, 'balnium Diaboli', is melancholy.

Since Beckett was one of the first writers I ever discovered for myself, some of his work is so embedded in my brain that I was also reminded of *Lessness*, a piece I first heard on the radio when I was a teenager. 'One step in the ruins in the sand on his back in the endlessness he will make it.' Teenagers love that stuff.

When I first read Beckett it seemed that the 'action' of his works took place in a timeless present, with no reference to past or future. These days it's broadly accepted that the 'universality' of Beckett's work is firmly rooted in his personal experience, particularly, in the case of *Waiting for Godot*, in the realities of his life in France under the German Occupation in World War II. The waiting that Estragon and Vladimir do has a lot in common with waiting for some word or signal from the French Resistance, of which Beckett was a part. Equally, the fictional ditches and barns in which Beckett's tramps hide or sleep are closely related to the actual ones that he and his partner Suzanne Dechevaux-Dumesnil made use of during their terrifying six-week journey, on foot, from Paris to the Unoccupied Zone in Burgundy, a journey made necessary after their Resistance cell was exposed by a double agent. 'I have changed refuge so often, in the course of my rout, that now I can't tell between dens and ruins,' a narrator says in 'The Calmative' from 1946.

In France in the 1940s there was no need for literary, metaphorical or symbolic ruins. Beckett had direct experience of the real thing, both during and after the war, as he described in a prose piece, originally a script for Radio Erin, titled 'The Capital of Ruins', a name given to the Normandy city of Saint-Lô, a place Beckett had come to know. In fact the city had a long history of ruin, having been destroyed by (among others) the Vikings in the ninth century and the English in the Hundred Years War, before being occupied by the German army in 1940 and all but totally destroyed by 'liberating' Allied bombing in 1944. Beckett encountered these final ruins in the second half of 1945, after the war had ended.

He had volunteered for the Irish Red Cross, which was helping to set up a hospital unit in the bombed city. His fluency in French allowed him to deal with the local authorities, and he was assigned the job of interpreter and storekeeper. In early August 1945 he travelled by sea aboard the *Menapia*, along with 350 tons of supplies, from Dublin to Cherbourg. His first job was to supervise the transfer of those supplies from the ship on to vehicles that then made the fifty-mile journey to Saint-Lô, through a devastated landscape, scarred with bomb craters, strewn with chunks of destroyed or abandoned machinery, and laced with land mines. Beckett's biographer, Deirdre Bair, writes, 'Everything was reduced to rubble so fine that when they were able to joke, they laughed that even the rubble had been reduced to rubble.'

By the time Beckett arrived in Saint-Lô some enterprising local photographer and publisher had already printed a booklet of before-and-after pictures of the city; the booklet's title was *Capitale des Ruines, 5 et 7 June 1944*, those being the dates of the Allied bombings. As far as I can tell, this commercialisation of ruins was a comparatively rare enterprise in World War II. There are a great many picture postcards from World War I showing French ruins and I've amassed a small collection without much difficulty; there are far fewer from World War II, though there were certainly postcards of Pearl Harbor after the Japanese attack. My guess is that in the 1914–18 conflict those images of ruin were thought likely to stir the hearts of patriots but by 1939–45 nobody had much confidence that they were likely to have the same effect.

Shortly after his arrival, Beckett wrote to his friend Thomas McGreevy: 'St-Lô is just a heap of rubble, la Capitale des Ruines as they call it in France. Of 2600 buildings 2000 completely wiped out . . . It has been raining hard for the last few days and the place is a sea of mud. What it will be like in winter is hard to imagine.' Other accounts actually put the level of destruction higher than Beckett did, estimating that ninety-five per cent of all the buildings were destroyed or damaged. The cathedral was left roofless, with much of its interior devastated, although Catholic mass was nevertheless celebrated in the ruins, not that Beckett would have participated.

One of Beckett's ancillary duties, towards the end of his time there, was driving to Dieppe to meet one Matron Mary Cowley, who was arriving by boat, and to drive her back to Saint-Lô through the devastated landscape. He managed this difficult task, and the pair arrived just as mass was being said in the cathedral. Deirdre Bair again:

> On the fringe of the candlelight, the ruins gleamed in the ghostly shadows. Beckett stood stiffly while Matron Cowley knelt and prayed. She sensed his discomfort and spared him her verbal gratitude when the mass was ended . . . Early the next morning when she tried to find him to thank him, Matron Cowley was told that he had gone back to Paris before dawn.

He wrote 'The Capital of the Ruins' the following year. It is an unusual text for Beckett, and would have been even stranger as a piece for Radio Erin, I think, and although there's some doubt about its exact history, it seems most likely that it was commissioned but never broadcast. That's not altogether surprising.

It begins as a piece of heightened literary reportage, describing the Irish Hospital in Saint-Lô, with some sharp journalistic observations, such as the walls of the operating theatre being lined with 'aluminium of aeronautic origin' which he considers 'a pleasant variation on the sword and ploughshare metamorphosis'. But his final sentiments, and certainly the language in which they're couched, would surely have been extraordinary hard for any radio listener to follow. He writes of 'the possibility that some of those who were in Saint-Lô will come home realising that they got at least as good as they gave, that they got indeed what they could hardly give, a vision and sense of a time-honoured conception of humanity in ruins, and perhaps even an inkling of the terms in which our condition is to be thought again.' Well, we might wonder just how many of those who were in Saint-Lô actually came away with a time-honoured vision of humanity in ruins (Matron Mary Cowley presumably did not), but evidently at least one did.

* * *

Beckett's fictional walkers, who walk in ruins, are themselves ruined, and Beckett was well aware of the dangers of walking even before the war. In 1938 he was walking at night in Paris with a group of friends when he was approached by a pimp, offering his services. Beckett declined, with some vehemence it's got to be assumed, and the pimp was so insulted that he stabbed Beckett in the chest, perforating a lung and very nearly killing him. The pimp, called Prudent, was briefly incarcerated, and Beckett didn't simply not press charges, he even went to visit him in prison, where the pimp was unable to explain his motivation – 'Je ne sais pas.' Later in his life Beckett, according to some reports, would recount the event as a comic anecdote, which would certainly be one way of dealing with it, though probably not a complete solution.

James Knowlson, who was one of the editors of *Beckett Remembering/Remembering Beckett*, tells us that many decades after the stabbing, he and Beckett were walking in the street near the old people's home where Beckett was then living, when a man with a camera leapt out and took a couple of photographs. Beckett, says Knowlson, reacted as though he'd been stabbed.

By that point in history there had been any number of performances of Beckett's plays in prisons, both by visiting theatre companies and by prisoners themselves. Rick Cluchey's San Quentin Drama Workshop was founded in 1958, a year after the Actor's Workshop of San Francisco had performed *Waiting for Godot* in the prison. As far as I can tell, there was never a production in Alcatraz.

Prisoners inevitably understand the nature of waiting but plenty of others, especially in places of conflict or political repression, understand it too. Performances of Beckett's work in apartheid South Africa seemed to assert the political dimension of his drama. Susan Sontag mounted a production of *Waiting for Godot* in Sarajevo in 1993, during the siege, a production which admittedly Kevin Myers in the *Daily Telegraph* called 'mesmerisingly precious and hideously self-indulgent', and then he became rather less kind. Even so, Beckett's work starts to look 'universal' all over again.

* * *

In April 2012, after the conflict in Syria had been going on for about a year, the BBC News website ran an article titled 'How *Waiting for Godot* offers Syrians hope'. It came with a photograph of a man walking through a ruined city street, framed by a collapsed concrete shopfront. The article was written by Ian Pannell and it described his meeting with a Syrian civilian from Idlib province whom he referred to as Abu Mohammed, though we were told that was not his real name. Government forces had attacked Idlib, left much of it in ruin, and then ground troops had moved in and, among a mass of other destructive acts, had deliberately set fire to Abu Mohammed's apartment. He was quoted as saying, 'I had five hundred books – English novels and plays, American poetry – and all of them are gone . . . If they burned all my home it's OK, but not my books – I cried when I saw my books.'

It turned out that *Waiting for Godot* was Abu Mohammed's favourite play. For him it was about hope. 'I believe Godot is hope,' he was quoted as saying, and I've spent a lot of time wondering if this interpretation makes any sense. In Beckett's play, Vladimir and Estragon already have hope: they hope that Godot will arrive. The hope is not in doubt, it's a question of whether those hopes will ever be realised, whether the thing they're waiting for will ever arrive.

But the more I think about it, the more I want Abu Muhammed's interpretation to make sense. The 'obvious' thing to have hoped for might be peace, justice, freedom, the defeat of Assad's forces, but perhaps the situation was so bad in Syria that he didn't even dare to hope for anything quite so ambitious. Perhaps he was hoping for hope to arrive, and then he would be able to hope for something more specific. He was hoping to have something to hope for. I think Samuel Beckett would have appreciated that. He certainly offered an appropriate line in *Company*, a prose piece from 1980, later put on the stage, 'Better hope deferred than none.'

In any case, all of this seemed rather lost on the BBC scribe who ended his article with a conclusion about the Syrian people: 'And after decades of what they see as state-sanctioned oppression rebellion burns bright – as they wait for Godot.' Spoiler alert Ian, Godot doesn't arrive. More than that, the tone of the BBC piece seemed to find it surprising that a Syrian should be familiar with the works of Samuel Beckett. Personally I was not surprised. I used to know, and go walking with, a Syrian who was a Beckett specialist.

In what now seems like another life, I had ambitions to be a man of the theatre, a writer and director rather than a performer, and I know that once (pretentiously, unironically, and instantly regretted) I expressed the ambition to become a *metteur en scène*. I imagined I might be a figure somewhere between Harold Pinter and Robert Wilson, a writer of dangerously crisp dialogue combined with grand avant-garde stage effects in the manner of performance art. You can imagine how well that turned out.

But before the scales fell from my eyes I studied for a one-year MA in European Drama at the University of Essex, in Colchester, where one of my fellow students was a Syrian named Kamal. Colchester itself has some very fine Roman ruins, including the Balkerne Gate, invariably referred to as 'the most complete Roman town gateway in Britain'. Essex University, however, was on a campus some way out of the city centre, and, in those days anyway, resembled a concrete slum. Some of the students, Kamal and I included, lived in student accommodation between the two, perhaps a mile and half from the campus. There was a city bus service that ran to the campus, and my student grant contained an extra allowance to cover a daily bus trip there and back. It occurred to me, and not only to me, that if a person walked to and from the campus and pocketed the bus allowance, he or she would come out ahead, so that's what I and many others did.

I never knew what Kamal's financial situation was, I assumed he had a grant from somewhere, but I imagined it was small, and certainly he saved money like the rest of us by walking to and from the university, and often we walked together. Today I can think of a thousand and one things I should have asked him about his life and his country but the truth is we mostly discussed European drama, with particular reference to Samuel Beckett. However, one thing I did learn about Kamal was that spending time in England studying drama was a way of avoiding the Syrian draft, or at least minimising his remaining stint, since he'd certainly done some military service already. The deal was that he would come to Essex to study first for an MA, and then complete a PhD, with Samuel Beckett as his main focus. This was scheduled to take four years, and if all went well and he was awarded his degrees, he would return to Syria and teach English literature at the University of Aleppo. If things didn't go well, if for any reason he didn't get his degrees, he'd return to Syria and do an extra two years in the army for each of the years he'd spent in Colchester. You might have thought that was quite an incentive to work hard at your Beckett studies, but it wasn't incentive enough.

Unlike Abu Mohammed in Idlib, my friend Kamal did not find a message of hope in *Waiting for Godot*, or in any of the other works of Samuel Beckett. He found a message of despair. As the days passed, and as we walked to and from campus together, Kamal embraced other Beckettian notions, that 'they gave birth astride a grave', that 'the only sin is the sin of being born', and so forth.

Kamal became increasingly morose and anguished, and then he began to drink. Walks to campus in the mornings were blighted by Kamal's metaphysical hangovers, walks back to student accommodation at night became wildly unsteady. To be fair, Kamal was by no means the only person following this pattern, but while so many of the students were just playing at it, Kamal's drinking, and his despair, were of a serious, cosmic, self-destructive, and in the end I would say actually not especially Beckettian kind. The general feeling was that a good man was falling into ruin.

In fact Samuel Beckett sometimes walked with a serious drinker or 'tippler' as he preferred to call him. The tippler was James Joyce: 'We walk through ourselves, meeting robbers, ghosts, giants, old men, young men, wives, widows, brothers-in-love. But always meeting ourselves.' In *Beckett Remembering/ Remembering Beckett*, Beckett recalled how, when he and Joyce both lived in Paris, he would sometimes get a phone call from the great man:

> And it was always to do with going for a walk or going for dinner. I remember a memorable walk on the Île des Cygnes with Joyce. And then he'd start his 'tippling' . . . We'd drink in any old pub or café. I don't remember which . . . And I brought him home drunk one night, but I won't go into that. He drank a lot but in the evenings only.

Kamal didn't show such restraint.

The MA in European drama had a practical element. The dozen or so miscellaneous students on the course arrived on campus in October and had to put on a theatrical production by the end of term, in December. A bit of Brecht or Strindberg was generally reckoned to be a sound choice, but we were having none of that. If ever a rabble of drama students was going to be free to do whatever the hell they liked theatrically, in a well-equipped theatre, with a small but adequate budget, and no 'adult' supervision, it was now. Who was going to waste an opportunity like that by doing a production of *Mother Courage*?

I put forward the idea that we should improvise a work from scratch, and in it we would express, individually and collectively, our own deepest fantasies and anxieties, our fears, and yes our hopes too. The idea was that by some magic this would become a sublimely inventive and moving dramatic performance, perhaps in the style of Peter Brook's 'total theatre'. Nobody even mocked me for this notion.

We even began doing group improvisation workshops in which we discussed the things that moved and inspired us most. We described and acted out favourite activities. I said how much I liked walking, but I wasn't sure how we'd put that on stage. We discussed using a treadmill, and yes, we could see the theatrical and symbolic possibilities of that. Some stage scenery depicting ruins would have been perfectly easy to arrange. We brought in our favourite pieces of text, favourite images, favourite sounds – which by no means had to be conventionally musical.

Kamal, in his gloom, was not the most exuberant participant in these sessions but he did finally say that he had a favourite sound, though it wasn't one that he could bring into the rehearsal room. It was the sound made by an artillery rocket being fired from its launcher. He knew this sound from the time he'd already spent in the Syrian army.

Rather a silence fell over the drama workshop after he said that. We were all liberals of course, we were all anti war, we were especially anti the launching of rockets against, well against anybody really, and clearly Kamal's favourite sound of the rocket being launched would be followed sooner or later by the sound of the rocket hitting its target, causing the destruction of somebody or something, creating ruin. Even if Kamal had only launched rockets as part of his training, as an exercise, this was nevertheless the rehearsal for a performance that was never going to be simply theatre.

We let him off the hook. We were embarrassed and feeble. We should, as we knew even then, have pinned him down, tried to make him talk it through. We might, at the very least, have enquired how he felt about delivering ruin to his enemies, and who these enemies might be. We had not imagined they would be other Syrians.

We abandoned our grand theatrical project, not because of Kamal's love of belligerent sounds but rather because, though I wouldn't have worded it quite this way at the time, we feared it might be mesmerisingly precious and hideously self-indulgent.

* * *

I'm sorry to say that I don't know the end of Kamal's story. A lot of fruitless enquiries to the university, much Googling and contacting of people I hoped might still be in touch with him, have left me none the wiser about whether he abandoned his Beckett studies and had to spend a great many years in the Syrian army, or whether he sobered up, pulled himself together and became a teacher of English literature at Aleppo University. It's perfectly possible, of course, that even if he did complete his PhD he might still have been dragged back into the military: all the evidence suggests that the Syrian Government under Basher al-Assad has never been very good at keeping promises to its people.

This is also to say that at the time of writing I don't know the end of the Syrian story either. I continue to follow the war in Syria distantly, as well as I can. In print and online there are still a lot of news images of ruin. These are shocking and appalling and frequently very beautiful. The images don't only show bombed and ruined buildings, more often than not they contain a figure walking through the aftermath, just like the one taken in Sheffield in the blitz. Frequently it will be a young man dressed in Western clothes, though sometimes it may be a man in white robes, and sometimes it's a man in camouflage carrying an automatic rifle. Occasionally it will be a woman or child. Once in a while it appears to be a looter, laden down with booty.

I find these still images far more moving than any of the shaky, hand-held video-footage, however immediate and urgent that footage may be. I know that in the case of the stills, the photographer must have waited patiently, anxiously, watching the ruins, anticipating the moment when a walker would come into his sights, and then when one did, he had fired the shutter, like a sniper, when the figure was in precisely the right, picturesque spot. Are some of these images 'Beckettian'? Well of course they are.

Aleppo is one of the oldest inhabited sites in the world, layered with multiple ruins of previous civilisations. Prior to the start of the war, Unesco was fretting that these ruins were threatened by the city's over-population: now this is no longer the main concern. In due course, 'security forces' stormed and bombed the university. The Syrian army also shelled Aleppo's ancient citadel, and in April 2013 the eleventh-century minaret of the Great Mosque was destroyed – each side blaming the other. Meanwhile, across the whole country, not only are new ruins being created and ancient ruins destroyed, but the latter are being stripped by grave robbers and looters.

Numbers in these situations are always imprecise and contestable, and never tell the whole truth, but it was estimated that by the mid 2013 a million and a half people had left Syria, finding their way into Jordan, Lebanon, Iraq, Egypt and Turkey. The last of these is the most obvious destination for refugees from Aleppo: it's only about thirty miles from the border. No doubt they get there by any method they can, but some undoubtedly must walk there.

Looking at the images of Syria in ruins and also at its walkers, I have never seriously entertained the idea that I will see my old friend Kamal walking through the rubble, another Molloy or Bellacqua. It would be satisfying in a way, but surely far too neat, too glib. There is also the possibility that having messed up his career as a Beckett scholar Kamal might have become a career soldier and ended up on the wrong side of the argument, still reading Beckett perhaps but also savouring the theatrical sound of rockets being fired, bringing ruin to his enemies.

* * *

It's strange how often the metaphor of the zombie, the walking dead, crops up in accounts of the Syrian conflict. Reporting on that bombing of the university, CNN described how

> Simon, an Aleppo University dental student, ran to help a young woman he saw walking zombie-like and clearly injured. He shouted to her and reached out. 'I came to hold her hand . . . to help her . . . ' Simon said. 'It came off . . . I was holding her dismembered hand in mine.'

A website named *The Revolting Syrian*, supporting the rebels, ran the headline, 'Like Zombies from a Horror Movie – Assad's Forces Raid a Children's School and Arrest the Boys.' There was a video clip on the site but it had been removed by the time I got to it, so I had to rely on the commentary:

> You can hear the screams of the girls inside the school as the film shows Assad's forces – faceless zombies here to collect their blood for Assad . . . Only in Syria can you send your child to school and have him never come back again. Lost in some dungeon of hell for eternity.

7

The Ruins of London, the Walk of the Worlds, the Last Psychogeographer on Earth, the Fall of the Arch of Usher, Walking into the Sunset - with Vampires and a Dog

These crumbling walls; these tottering arcades;
These mouldering plinths; these sad, and blacken'd shafts;
These vague entablatures; this broken frieze;
These shattered cornices; this wreck; this ruin;
These stones, alas! – these grey stones – are they all –
All of the great and the colossal left
By the corrosive hours to Fate and me?

Edgar Allan Poe, *The Coliseum*

Ambition sigh'd: She found in vain to trust
The faithless column, and the crumbling bust:

Alexander Pope, *Epistle to Mr Addison*

After five years in Italy you become a monument. After ten years, you become a relic. And after twenty years, you become a ruin.

Gore Vidal

There's a story, true as far as I know, that when Roger Corman was in the middle of shooting *House of Usher* (1960) – one of his eight Edgar Allan Poe movie adaptations, all but one of them starring Vincent Price – he heard that a house had just burned down in the Hollywood Hills. He quickly assembled a small crew and filmed Mark Damon, as Philip Winthrop, riding a horse through the ruined landscape. These shots form the opening of the movie.

Since Poe's story takes place in an unspecified gothic neverland, who's to say that setting didn't look much like the Hollywood Hills, a place where I do a certain amount of walking? But in fact that opening sequence is filmed from a very high angle, the camera pointing downwards, revealing no horizon or hilltop, and showing a landscape so generic that you could easily think it was filmed on a back lot or sound stage. There's certainly no way that having watched the movie, you could locate that ruined landscape, go there, poke around, and be able to say that you'd walked where Corman's House of Usher once stood. I find that a great shame.

Both the film and Poe's story *The Fall of the House of Usher* conflate the ruin of a building with the ruin of the human body. And when I walk in the Hollywood Hills these days, feeling the occasional twinge in the back or knees, finding that the lungs don't pump oxygen with quite the efficiency they used to, it would be good to feel I might come across an identifiable landscape that, in however fictional and oblique a way, I could relate to and see as the fictional and cinematic equivalent of my ever older, ever less reliable, even more ruined body.

* * *

Like the narrator of Samuel Beckett's 'First Love', I willingly take the air in graveyards. I like walking in cemeteries, in town and country, at home and abroad. They don't absolutely have to be ruined, but I much prefer it when they are. A well-tended, well-ordered cemetery signifies dignity and respect, but when things have started to slide, when the ground has shifted, the headstones tilted, when ruin and entropy have started to reassert themselves, that's when a graveyard really comes alive.

And when you walk in ruined graveyards you often see other walkers, and they seldom look as though they're there to visit anyone's grave, and you think, 'Well, he must be up to no good, skulking around the graves in the middle of the day, nothing better to do, an idler, a ne'er-do-well,' and of course you realise he (and it usually is a he) may well be thinking exactly the same thing about you. And as well as walkers, the more disordered graveyards tend to have a few people sitting or sometimes lying around, usually experiencing the effects of cheap alcohol, sometimes to the point of unconsciousness. Personally, I try to avoid that, mostly.

I was walking in Abney Park Cemetery in Hackney, east London, a place dating back to the eighteenth century that was a park before it was a cemetery; then in 1840 it became a non-denominational garden cemetery and arboretum, complete with a chapel built in Dissenting Gothic style. These days it's designated an 'Historic Park and Garden', and a nature reserve, which means that the powers that be aren't going to do much of anything, thereby allowing nature to take its course, which in some respects means letting ruin and entropy reassert themselves. I'm all for this, naturally.

And so in Abney Park Cemetery I admired a fine array of displaced and overgrown graves and monuments, fallen headstones that had once been regimented, at attention, and had now stood down. There were broken columns and pieces of statuary, sometimes wreathed in carved foliage, sometimes wreathed in the real thing. There were some dead trees that hadn't fallen down yet, though there were also lumps of decaying roots from ones that had, stacked alongside miscellaneous bits of graveyard masonry. There was a wall painted with the message, 'We R Legion. Turn Back.'

I didn't turn back. I went to get a closer look at the old chapel. This was a genuine ruin, and a kind of wonder, a folly to be sure, tall and thin, rigorously symmetrical, a long, slender spire, turrets, a rose window: a fairytale castle, or perhaps the fortress where the maiden might once have been kept. And there was now something even more fortress-like about it, though the

intention was to keep people out rather than in: doorways were filled in with breeze blocks, some windows were boarded up with sheets of wood, some covered with corrugated sheet metal, though one or two of these had been prised open a little, and a large bird's nest was visible behind one of them.

English Heritage declares this to be a place in peril, a building at risk. There are plans that involve investment, restoration, local skills training and improved access. I didn't know any of this at the time – I did my research retrospectively – though I could probably have guessed, and I'm certainly not sure it would have improved my experience any. It surely wouldn't have done much for the couple I encountered on one of the cemetery's more obscure paths.

It was a man and a woman, not so very old, probably in their mid-thirties, though they looked like they'd lived pretty hard. Were they ruined? Well, they certainly looked damaged. She was sitting, he was standing, and each of them held a litre bottle of wine, both about three quarters consumed, and although I could only guess what these people's relationship was, how well they knew each other, if at all, I could hear that some kind of erotic negotiation was taking place. The obvious thought was that the woman might be offering her services for a price, but that didn't seem to be what was going on. Whether money was changing hands I couldn't say, but the woman was obviously more enthusiastic and insistent about the transaction than the man. He was thoroughly reluctant and I distinctly heard him say, 'I'll give you a few minutes of this and that, but that's all I'm prepared to do.'

Maybe he just didn't fancy her, or perhaps he was suffering from pre-performance anxiety and didn't want to get her hopes up. A man with, at least, three quarters of a litre of wine inside him might not be confident about his ability to function as anybody's dream-date.

* * *

I was in Abney Park Cemetery following, rather distantly, in the footsteps of Edgar Allan Poe. It seems more than likely he set foot there at some time, though before the park became a cemetery. One of the park's entrances is in Stoke Newington Church Street, which was also the location of the boarding school where Poe briefly lived and was educated, at the Reverend John Bransby's Manor House School, before John Allan and his wife, his adoptive parents, took him back to America. This was in 1820, when he was eleven years old.

The school is long gone and there's now a wine bar on the site, the Fox Reformed. The phrases *specialités de vins fins* and *aperitifs de marque* were painted on the windows when I made my visit. The urge to class things up with a bit of foreign language is as alive today as it was in Poe's fiction. There's a bust of Poe high on the wall above the wine bar, and a commemorative plaque which was unveiled by Steven Berkoff, creator and star of dramatisations of Poe's *The Tell-Tale Heart* and *The Fall of the House of Usher*, which is no doubt why he got the unveiling gig.

As I stood looking up at the bust of Poe, a friend of a friend happened to be walking along the street, a former rock-group manager now a local librarian, and I explained what I was doing there. 'Ah,' he said, unprompted, 'you're on a drift.' Thus the language of psychogeography spreads around the world like a contagion.

* * *

In the corner shops and bus stations, people may not necessarily be talking about the Situationists (the begetters of psychogeography), but in the hipper university departments they seem to talk of little else. Sometimes described as anarchists, sometimes as Libertarian Marxists, the Situationists (as far as I can tell there were never more than ten of them) were active from the late 1950s to the early 1970s in France. They and their leader Guy Debord (who expelled each of the other members till he was the only one left) devised various strategies to subvert capitalist society, believing (uncontroversially it seems to me) that individuals should construct the 'situations' of their own lives.

Psychogeography was one of these strategies, and the drift, or *dérive*, was one of the tactics. '*Dérives* involve playful-constructive behavior and awareness of psychogeographical effects, and are thus quite different from the classic notions of journey or stroll' (Debord, 'The Theory of the *Dérive*', published in the magazine *Situationiste Internationale*, 1958).

Most of the time I'm not so sure that a drift is really 'quite different' at all. The idea of walking through cities and looking at things in new or surprising ways is surely as old as cities themselves. But the practice did reach a kind of apotheosis in nineteenth-century France with the rise of the *flâneur*, literally stroller, but with overtones of the man about town, the urban explorer, and idler.

Baudelaire championed the *flâneur*:

> The crowd is his element, as the air is that of birds and water of fishes ... For the perfect *flâneur*, for the passionate spectator, it is an immense joy to set up house in the heart of the multitude, amid the ebb and flow of movement, in the midst of the fugitive and the infinite.' ['The Painter of Modern Life', first published in *Le Figaro* in 1863.]

Since Baudelaire was also the translator of Poe, it was natural that he should look for evidence of the *flâneur* in Poe's work and he found it in the short story 'The Man of the Crowd'. Poe wrote it at pretty much the same time that Abney Park was being turned into a cemetery; it was published simultaneously in 1840 in two Philadelphia journals: *Burton's Gentleman's Magazine* (of which Poe was the editor) and *Atkinson's Casket.*

Walter Benjamin was a big fan of this story too, writing that it 'is something like the X-ray picture of a detective story. In it, the drapery represented by crime has disappeared. The mere armature has remained: the pursuer, the crowd, and an unknown man who arranges his walk through London in such a way that he always remains in the middle of the crowd.' Some might argue that really wasn't all that much of an armature.

For some, 'The Man of the Crowd' is a crucial text in the history of modernist fiction, and in the literature of pedestrianism *per se*, and sometimes I think that's exactly what the story is, but at other times I'm not so sure. The plot itself won't delay us long: one man follows another through the streets of London for a very long time, for no very good reason. He seem like a distant, early predecessor of Sophie Calle.

At the beginning of the story, Poe's unnamed narrator sits in the window of a London coffee house, within a hotel, watching the world and its people go by. He's recovering from an illness and finds the spectacle both fascinating and alarming, and is finally struck by a single 'devilish' face belonging to an old man whom he feels compelled to follow. The pursuit continues as the old man walks through London, apparently with purpose, though that purpose becomes increasingly indiscernible.

It's a walk on the ruined wild side: 'wooden tenements were seen tottering to their fall . . . horrible filth festered in the dammed-up gutters . . . large bands of the most abandoned of a London populace were seen reeling to and fro.' Nothing unfamiliar there to a contemporary Londoner, then. Poe's old man has a 'wild energy', and doesn't slow down. And neither, improbably, does the sickly narrator, who tracks him for the rest of the night, and all of the next day until, as the 'shades of the second evening are coming on', he's finally had enough and gives up the chase. Our narrator concludes, 'this old man is the type and the genius of deep crime. He refuses to be alone. He is the man of the crowd . . . I shall learn no more of him, nor of his deeds.'

For me, it's one of those stories that keeps slipping in and out of focus. Sometimes it really does seem sublimely prescient of so much modern literature (think Borges, Thomas Pynchon, Paul Auster, *et al.*), a mystery that refuses to be solved, that refuses even to reveal its nature. I know there are many supporters for this view. Other times I wonder if Poe didn't simply write himself into a corner, realised he couldn't resolve his story, couldn't find a 'solution' that would be equal to the intensity of the quest, and so he inverted and subverted the narrative; now the mystery is too profound to be understood, or perhaps the mystery is that there's no mystery at all. (This is the kind of things that gets pretty short shrift in Hollywood script meetings, let me tell you.) There's also some possibility that the narrator never actually leaves the coffee house at all, and that the narrative takes place entirely in his fevered imagination. Ditto.

As far as I can tell 'The Man of the Crowd' has never been turned into a 'real' movie (though IMDb, the Internet Movie

Database, lists a video short), which is frankly a surprise. What was Roger Corman up to? Didn't he think the story measured up to his usual high standards?

Poe had been away from London for twenty years when he wrote 'The Man of the Crowd', so he didn't have much direct, personal experience of the city to go on; it's generally reckoned that his version of London is actually cribbed from Dickens. No actual London districts or place names are mentioned in the story. The hero is staying in the D— Hotel, which I've always imagined to be in Piccadilly, a street with plenty of opportunities for people watching. I admit I have no real basis for thinking this, but I'm making an association between Poe's old man with the devilish face and Bram Stoker's Count Dracula who had rooms there.

Some claims are made for Dracula as a psychogeographer, walking around the metropolis eyeing victims, and certainly the novel *Dracula* is packed with walking: in London, Transylvania and Whitby; and with ruin too: Whitby Abbey, a ruined castle, a ruined chapel, a 'ruined tomb in a forgotten land'. The current wisdom is that *Dracula* is a response to certain late-nineteenth-century British imperial anxieties. While the British Empire exerted its influence around large parts of the world, London, its capital and at that point the largest city the world had ever known (4.7 million inhabitants by 1900), was uniquely vulnerable to the pernicious morals, manners, and in some cases actual contagious diseases, brought in by 'aliens'. I've certainly walked along Piccadilly plenty of times, as a man in the crowd if not necessarily a man of the crowd, and I've looked at all the people walking around me, at all the unfamiliar and alien (in several senses of the word) faces, and wondered which ones might be geniuses of deep crime, which ones it might be fun to follow, and which ones are vampires.

The current wisdom detects much the same anxieties in

H. G. Wells's *The War of the Worlds*, published in the same year as *Dracula* – 1897. Wells is a little more on the side of the angels in his novel. His unnamed narrator recognises that the Martians treat the people of Britain with the same indifference and contempt that British colonisers direct against 'inferior races' (Wells's term, though he doesn't use quotation marks, alas). Conrad's *Heart of Darkness*, responding in a different way to similar anxieties, appeared two years later.

* * *

You'll find H. G. Wells quoted all over the place, especially on those dubious 'advice to entry-level writers' websites, as having said or written, 'I write as straight as I can, just as I walk as straight as I can, because that is the best way to get there.'

In fact the source is Wells's *An Experiment in Autobiography*, published in 1934, and it's not an entirely straightforward comment either about writing or walking. He's saying it to bad-mouth the prose style of Joseph Conrad, whom he finds fancy and over-literary. The quotation in full is, *'I write as I walk because I want to get somewhere* [my italics] and I write as straight as I can, just as I walk as straight as I can, because that is the best way to get there.'

To which the obvious response surely is: Well, that all depends on which 'somewhere' you're trying to get to, doesn't it? Certainly, a straight line is the shortest distance between two points, but if the two points are, say, either side of a river (think of Wellington at the Battle of Assaye), it might be wise to walk along the riverbank to a bridge or a ford, rather than just plunge straight in. For that matter, just how many paths, trails or walking routes are actually very straight? Roman roads aside, don't they at the very least twist and turn as they follow the basic topography of the landscape? There's also the issue that you don't need to be some damn *flâneur* to believe that walking isn't always simply about getting somewhere quickly and efficiently. A walk without an obvious goal is enjoyable in itself.

Writing is a trickier matter. Writing without having the slightest idea of where you're heading is probably not a great idea, but which writer hasn't been completely and thoroughly lost somewhere in the middle of a piece of writing? In any case, I'm not sure that 'straightness' is an absolute virtue in writing any more than in walking: it seems more like a stylistic choice. Wells chose straightness for the very good reason that if you're going to write speculative fiction or scientific romance, then a good plain prose style can help a lot with credibility and suspension of disbelief.

In fact there's evidence that Wells may have talked the talk rather differently than he walked the walk. A passage in Jerome K. Jerome's *My Life and Times* (1925) describes a visit to Wells's house in Sandgate, near Folkestone: Jerome had been under the weather and Wells invited him down to the coast for some sea air and a rest.

Jerome writes:

> To 'rest' in the neighbourhood of Wells is like curling yourself up and trying to go to sleep in the centre of a cyclone ... There are steepish hills on the South Downs. We went up them at four miles an hour, talking all the time. On the Sunday evening a hurricane was raging with a driving sleet. Wells was sure a walk would do us good – wake us up. While Mrs Wells was not watching, we tucked the two little boys into their mackintoshes and took them with us. 'We'll all have a blow,' said Wells.

It sounds to me like Wells was walking fast but in no particular direction, and setting off with the kids for an evening walk in driving sleet doesn't sound like it's the very best way to get anywhere whatsoever. Trust the gossip, not the teller.

That visit to Folkestone must have been in the early years of the twentieth century. Before that, Wells and his second wife, known as Jane, lived in a semi-detached house in Maybury Road, in Woking, Surrey, twenty-some miles south-west of London, a place later memorialised in the Jam's song 'A Town Called Malice'. Wells had just started to make a living as a writer. His mornings were spent walking, or sometimes cycling, in the nearby countryside; in the afternoons he wrote. Legend has it that he was walking with his brother on one of those mornings, and they imagined how it would be if Martians suddenly descended on this English scene and set about destroying it. Thus was born *The War of the Worlds*, a fine book full of walking and ruin.

The narrator of *The War of the Worlds* is 'much occupied in learning to ride the bicycle' and 'busy upon a series of papers discussing the probable developments of moral ideas as civilisation progressed'. It sounds like a full life, but he still finds time for pedestrianism. 'One night . . . I went for a walk with my wife. It was starlight and I explained the Signs of the Zodiac to her.' No word on whether the little woman thanked him for this.

Soon enough the Martians arrive, in cylinders, landing in the sandpits on Horsell Common, just outside Woking, and it takes a while before anything more ominous happens; but creatures duly emerge from the cylinders and begin building machines, or I suppose vehicles, what Wells calls 'walking engines'.

> And this Thing I saw: How can I describe it? A monstrous tripod, higher than many houses, striding over the young pine trees, and smashing them aside in its career; a walking engine of glittering metal, striding now across the heather.

Fortunately a member of the English working class is at hand to offer a more earthy description, 'Boilers on stilts, I tell you, striding along like men.'

We also get a description of the living Martians, each one a greyish hulk, about the size of a bear, glistening like wet leather, heaving and pulsating convulsively, dark-coloured eyes, a lipless mouth that quivers and drops saliva, and lank but wriggling tentacles. These do not sound like aliens well equipped for planetary conquest, but their tripods are armed with fearsome heat-rays.

Things don't go well for mankind: the Martians take over and destroy much of Woking and beyond. Finding himself stranded in the colonised Martian zone, our hero spends a lot of time dodging the tripods, holing up in a ruined house, and eventually doing some walking through a devastated and depopulated London and its suburbs. 'Scrambling over a ruined wall, [I] went on my way through scarlet and crimson trees towards Kew – it was like walking through an avenue of gigantic blood drops.'

Still, it all turns out all right in the end: the Martians catch something nasty and die ('slain by the . . . bacteria against which their systems were unprepared'); civilisation returns, and one of the last images in the book has our hero standing on Primrose Hill where he's able 'to see the people walking to and fro among the flowerbeds on the hill, to see the sightseers about the Martian machine that stands there still'. Being able to walk freely about the city is an emblem both of freedom and order.

The War of the Worlds contains two deeply disturbing and enduring narrative tropes. First, Wells imagines the destruction of his own neighbourhood, even his own street;

> I . . . crept towards the window. As I did so, the view opened out until, on the one hand, it reached to the houses about Woking station, and on the other to the charred and blackened pine woods of Byfleet. There was a light down below the hill, on the railway, near the arch, and several of the houses along the Maybury Road and the streets near the station were glowing ruins.

Then, after the Martians, like many new immigrants, have

moved from the outskirts to the centre, into London itself, the native population there moves out, is evacuated in this case, and Wells describes what the narrator calls 'Dead London'.

> Why was I wandering alone in this city of the dead? Why was I alone when all London was lying in state, and in its black shroud? I felt intolerably lonely . . . I came into Oxford Street by the Marble Arch, and here again were black powder and several bodies, and an evil, ominous smell from the gratings of the cellars of some of the houses.

This is great stuff, isn't it? Haven't we all imagined the destruction of our own neighbourhoods; haven't we all imagined being the only inhabitant of an abandoned city? Of course there are some people for whom these situations have been real rather than imaginary, although only in fiction have they had to contend with Martians or indeed vampires.

The War of the Worlds is not a vampire story, but the Martians are definitely vampires of a sort.

> They did not eat, much less digest. Instead, they took the fresh, living blood of other creatures, and injected it into their own veins. I have myself seen this being done, as I shall mention in its place. But, squeamish as I may seem, I cannot bring myself to describe what I could not endure even to continue watching. Let it suffice to say, blood obtained from a still living animal, in most cases from a human being, was run directly by means of a little pipette into the recipient canal . . .

* * *

When you step out of Woking railway station and start walking, the streets lead you through a short pedestrianised strip, named Crown Square, and at the end of it, where it meets Church Street East, you come upon a twenty-three-foot high, stainless-steel statue called 'Martian Walking Engine'. If this isn't too all-engrossing you may also notice a metal cylinder half-lodged in the ground, and certain paving stones that have biomorphic metal shapes set into them, officially referred to as 'bacteria slabs'. You're looking at a sculpture, or I suppose installation, by Michael Condron, inspired by *The War of the Worlds*.

In place since 1998, it is, by some way, the most fun piece of public art I have ever set eyes on, though it's not wholly benign. Three slender legs rise at irregular angles from the pavement, and meet to support a pod, a squashed sphere, that resembles a space capsule more than the boiler mentioned in the book. At the front of the pod there's a kind of windscreen through which the Martian could have gazed out, and tentacles dangle from the pod's underside. The overall result is wonderful, slick and shiny, streamlined and other-wordly, and while it probably doesn't actually give the kids nightmares, there's something genuinely unsettling about it.

I watched as people walked past and around the Martian, and sometimes under it, between its legs, but they seemed not to register its existence. I didn't even notice anybody looking up. I probably shouldn't have been surprised. If they were locals they'd no doubt seen it often enough not to find it remarkable: it was just a piece of street furniture, and perhaps an obstacle to their walking. But equally they didn't seem to find it odd that I had stopped to stand and stare, to walk around it, to see it from all angles. They must be used to that too.

It's always hard to imagine exactly how a tripod walks. Does it move one leg at a time, which seems a very slow and laborious process? Or does it move one leg and use that as a pivot as it brings the other two forward? That would be a quicker method of travel, but would surely cause a lot of instability. Wells really doesn't tell us much about how the Martian tripods get around. He says they stride and rush, and asks, 'Can you imagine a

milking stool tilted and bowled violently along the ground?' To which the answer is, well only up to a point.

Could Michael Condron's walking machine have ever actually walked? I'm not sure. The legs are enormously long and thin, but the thighs (as it were) are very short in relation to the calves. The thing would have wobbled hopelessly, not least because it doesn't have any feet. The legs simply disappear into the paving slabs. You could perhaps tell yourself that the feet, or claws, or stabilising pads, or whatever, had smashed through the pavement and were lurking unseen some way below the surface, but surely a thing that smashed into the ground with such force would scarcely have been able to get around at all. I didn't altogether blame the sculptor, adding feet of any sort would probably have spoiled the slender elegance of the design. On the other hand, a man who's interested in just how alien tripods could walk through the ruins of Woking was left asking himself a lot of questions.

* * *

I pondered these questions as I walked to Wells's old home, the semi-detached house in Maybury Road, a perfectly straight road that leads directly to the station; a commuter's dream. I still haven't decided whether it means anything, but I know that J. G. Ballard had an extraordinarily similar arrangement in Shepperton. He too lived in a semi-detached that was a short, straight walk from station, where you could catch a train that would take you up to the fleshpots of London, which Ballard, of course, as much as Wells, also imagined in ruins. Ballard wrote a piece of fiction titled 'The Autobiography of JGB' in which the narrator explores a wholly deserted London.

The War of the Worlds contains a chapter titled 'What I Saw of the Destruction of Weybridge and Shepperton'.

> The decapitated colossus reeled like a drunken giant; but it did not fall over. It recovered its balance by a miracle, and, no longer heeding its steps and with the camera that fired the Heat-Ray now rigidly upheld, it reeled swiftly upon Shepperton. The living intelligence, the Martian within the hood, was slain and splashed to the four winds of heaven,

> and the Thing was now but a mere intricate device of metal whirling to destruction. It drove along in a straight line, incapable of guidance. It struck the tower of Shepperton Church, smashing it down as the impact of a battering ram might have done, swerved aside, blundered on and collapsed with tremendous force into the river out of my sight.

This too is great stuff, but I'm not sure it's necessarily the 'straight' prose that Wells claimed to write: some of it sounds a little fancy to me.

There are houses on only one side of Maybury Road. The railway line runs along the other, on an embankment at about bedroom-window level. There's a fence and some shrubby trees, positioned between the street and the tracks, but it seems the trains must be far more visible than the residents want them to be. Lace curtains and high hedges shield many of the houses from the sight of passing trains.

When I went there I could see that Wells's house had been modernised a little more than many in the street. There was nothing that looked like a ruin, but one or two of the buildings were decaying gently. Wells's house had been newly rendered, given a PVC front door, and there was hard standing for a car in what had once been the front garden; but there's a limit to how much people can, or want to, change a basic semi.

My guess is that Wells wouldn't have found so very much to surprise him in this, for us contemporary, for him future, version of Maybury Road. Yes, there was a big yellow-painted garage offering 'Trade-price tyres direct to the public', and although there wouldn't have been many cars in Woking when Wells lived there in the last years of the nineteenth century, by the time he died in 1946 he'd have been familiar with the 'motor age'.

There was a modern printing works in the street too, named Optichrome, which sounds oddly Wellsian and Victorian to me.

He might have been more surprised by 'Libas, elegant Asian design', and the 'Body and Beauty Studio', run from adjacent houses, but it was hardly the kind of shock Wells's Time Traveller had to deal with. As visions of the future go, this was a modest one, and by Wells's standards positively mundane.

* * *

And so I left Wells's old house and street, and walked around Woking looking for signs of ruin. It wasn't easy to find any. Woking was a tidy and prosperous place. I knew there was a ruined abbey in the old part of town but that seemed too obvious. I was looking for modern, contemporary, or perhaps alien, ruin, and it was thin on the ground. Even the canal, generally a reliable source of wreckage and neglect, was here in excellent condition, clean water, exuberant vegetation, not a shopping trolley or dumped bicycle to be found.

There was a shuttered pub, one of the Rat and Parrot chain, windows and doors covered with corrugated sheet metal, but it looked like it could be spruced up easily enough by a new owner. Really, the best I could find was the old Woking Liberal Club. No longer in use, it was a chunky, out of the box, 1960s building: industrial components, concrete slabs, big glass windows, a less than welcoming entrance under a gloomy portico.

I subsequently discovered that it had been a taxi office after it was a club, and was about to be demolished and replaced by a block of flats. I don't think anybody was very concerned about this, though possibly one or two fans of the Jam may have regretted its passing. This, it turns out, was one of the first places the Jam rehearsed and played, back in the 1970s; Paul Weller lived round the corner in Stanley Road. I always felt that song 'A Town Called Malice' overstated the horrors of being a teenager in a small, dull town, especially one that's just half an hour's train ride from the fleshpots of London. Try being a teenager in Sheffield.

But perhaps this is an essential part of the suburban adolescent experience. You're disaffected to a greater or lesser degree. You want to see the known world swept away, a world that isn't yours. You walk (or mooch) the streets, feeling vaguely hostile, vaguely resentful, and you really wouldn't mind if these neat, safe, orderly little houses were reduced to ruins. Of course, some time later, you may walk the same or similar streets, and realise that life in these houses isn't nearly as neat, safe or orderly as you naïvely imagined it to be.

Here at the Liberal Club the 'street artists' of Woking had expressed their disaffection, if not in a very inspired way. They'd managed to get up to the first floor and sprayed faces, doodles and initials on the windows, inside and out. It was artless, but we've all seen worse. And at ground level, somebody had sprayed on the wall, in fact stencilled, the name 'Banksy'. Now, this was just sad. Yes, so the Woking lads knew that Banksy was a major figure, and they knew he sometimes stencilled his name, though not always, and in fact the style of the stencil here didn't look all that much like the authentic versions I'd seen. But hadn't it occurred to the Woking posse that Banksy actually attached his name to droll, witty, provocative imagery, and that there was none of that here? The name itself just wasn't enough. For that matter, didn't they know that in the world of street art, or even among taggers, it's a pretty heinous offence to sign somebody else's name? Isn't this the kind of thing that starts a 'bombing' war? Well, maybe not here. I dare say Banksy wasn't about to do a lightning raid to correct matters and take vengeance; not in Woking.

I turned and headed to Horsell Common, to the sandpits where Wells's Martians first landed in their cylinders, a couple of miles out of the centre of town. Horsell Common, as the unwary pedestrian, like me, soon finds out on a sweaty afternoon in late summer, and probably should have thought about in advance, is a vast expanse, covering the best part of nine hundred acres, laced with roaring, unforgiving arterial roads. Large parts of the common look like a bit of Scotland dropped into the heart of southern England; the heather that Wells mentioned is real enough. But here, even more than in the town, there was no sign of ruin. The landscape was remarkably tidy and well looked after. In the woods I came across a kind of hut made of tree branches, but it didn't look like it had ever been some traveller's hovel, not even a place where teenagers got up to minor forms of no good. It actually looked more like a well-made boy-scout project.

I didn't feel especially miffed or aggrieved about all this, but I did find things a bit disappointing. I didn't wish for the specific or general ruination of Woking, but given my project I couldn't help thinking that change and growth always requires a certain amount of decay. A degree of ruination is necessary and desirable in a city. I didn't want to walk through a Woking that had been reduced to a smouldering bomb-site, but I'd have welcomed some healthful decay, a few more gaps and blanks. Some things have to fall away before new things can come into being.

And then I saw something lurking in the shadowy undergrowth, something large, black and shiny. I couldn't see it very well, but from a distance it really did look like a metal cylinder, maybe an old oil drum on its side, I thought. But as I got nearer it moved, it really did. It seemed to heave and pulse. I got the shock of my life. And then it moved again. It didn't go anywhere, it stayed right where it was and it seemed to be breathing. And why wouldn't it? Horsell Common is open grazing land. My metallic alien cylinder was the body of a large, reclining, black, shiny cow.

* * *

Wells was hardly the first or last to imagine a ruined London, but the London of *The War of the Worlds* is ultimately restored, and that must surely have a lot to do with the book's enduring popularity. It has a feel-good ending, order is restored, and the good guys win, though admittedly not as a result of their own actions.

The fact that the aliens first land in some out-of-the-way place helps too. It would have been a very different and I think lesser book if Wells's aliens had descended and begun their destruction right in the middle of Piccadilly. Orson Welles appreciated this. His 1938 Mercury Theater radio broadcast had the aliens land in the unincorporated village of Grover's Mill, in New Jersey, before they moved into New York City.

The script, by Howard Koch and Anne Froelick, seems pretty corny to a modern reader, and it's hard to believe that many Americans were actually deceived into thinking the invasion was real.

> 'Wait a minute . . . Enemy now in sight above the Palisades. Five – five great machines. First one is crossing the river. I can see it from here, wading the Hudson like a man wading through a brook . . . Now the smoke's spreading faster. It's reached Times Square. People trying to run away from it, but it's no use. They're falling like flies.'

H. G. Wells himself had doubts about how much panic the broadcast really caused. Incredibly, a recording exists of a meeting between Wells and Welles at a radio station in San Antonio two years after the Mercury Theater broadcast. At that point, of course, the war in Europe had started, though the USA was still some way away from having aliens launch an attack on Pearl Harbor.

In the radio conversation, Wells, who sounds avuncular, roguish, and a little condescending towards his almost namesake, says, 'Are you sure there was such a panic in America, or wasn't it your Halloween fun?' Orson dodges the question, and says,

'Mr Hitler made a good deal of sport of it, in the great Munich speech, you know . . . and it's supposed to show the corrupt condition and decadence [*sic*] state of affairs in democracies that *The War of the Worlds* went over as well as it did. I think it's very nice of Mr Wells to say that not only I didn't mean it but the American people didn't mean it.'

Even so, I suppose there must have been *some* people who really did believe what they heard on the radio, and you can see how annoying and humiliating that would have felt after the event; and certain other people, or possibly the same ones, may have thought that later reports of Pearl Harbor were a fiction in the same vein, or so it was reported, though frankly these reports seem even harder to swallow.

And what to make of stories concerning a broadcast by the Ecuadorian station Radio Quito of their version of *The War of the Worlds* in 1949, based on a 1946 Chilean script, a show that came without disclaimers, and interrupted regular programmes, as actors described the landing of aliens about twenty miles outside the city? Accounts have it that there was immediate panic in the streets of Quito, and when the station revealed the broadcast to be a piece of drama, and appealed for calm, the panic turned into a full-blown riot. Annoyance and humiliation can affect an audience that way. A mob apparently descended on the radio station, housed in the same building as *El Comercio*, the national newspaper, and with a hundred or so employees still inside, the place was torched. It's said that the citizens of Quito were perfectly willing to believe they'd been invaded, but nobody really thought the aliens had come from Mars, they thought they'd come from Peru.

* * *

As all this suggests, the terrors, and indeed the plot, of *The War of the Worlds* are transferable, and can be moved far beyond the boundaries of London and England. Steven Spielberg's 2005 movie purported to be set, at least initially, in New Jersey, though parts of it were filmed all over America, including (according to IMDb) one scene shot at the corner of Witmer Street and Ingraham Street, in MacArthur Park, Los Angeles, streets that I walked along all the time when I used to have business at the Good Samaritan Hospital a couple of blocks away. Close readers will be interested to note that Spielberg's movie is titled *War of the Worlds*, ditching the initial *The*.

However, the 1953 movie version, produced by George Pal, directed by Byron Haskin, is the only one to set the action resolutely in California, with the Martians touching down in the fictional town of Linda Rosa (actually the real town of Corona), before moving into Los Angeles proper and destroying much of the city, including most spectacularly the City Hall building on Spring Street. Again the hero, who now has a name, Dr Clayton Foster, played by Gene Barry (you know he's smart because he wears glasses: you know he's tough because he wears a leather jacket), at one point finds himself alone, walking in a dead, evacuated city.

Inevitably, the success of the movie was due largely to the special effects and the gorgeously designed Martian flying (not walking) machines, supposedly based on the manta ray, though in fact having a lot in common with 1950s automotive design. But there are some very effective and affecting scenes of people trying to bribe or fight their way on to trucks to get out of the city, with the hero finally left in the deserted downtown streets. Some of this does look as though it was filmed on a back lot, and much use is made of miniatures, but some parts are definitely filmed in a genuinely empty downtown. In one shot the street signs for 8th Street and Hill are clearly visible in the foreground, with a sign for the Fruit of the Loom company on a building behind.

The current wisdom is that Pal's movie is a response to certain mid-twentieth-century American imperial anxieties. America had won the 'real' war, was the strongest power on the planet, yet found itself in the middle of a Cold War against what had been one of its allies. Being in possession of the atomic bomb delivered neither security nor control, and in the movie it's useless against the Martians; the nuclear explosions leave them unblemished, and nobody frets about fallout.

Whether Pal's Martians are vampires is hard to tell: it's not the kind of movie to be much concerned with the digestive system of the invaders. But, staying true to the novel, victory comes far more by good luck than good management, as again the Martians are killed by bacteria.

* * *

Those who found this an unrealistic or over-optimistic outcome, might have been more persuaded by Richard Matheson's novel *I Am Legend*, published in 1954, a post-apocalyptic novel in which the world has been ruined by a virus and the vast majority of the world's population turned into vampires. The hero, Robert Neville, lives in his own house on Cimarron Street, in Gardena, a city in Los Angeles county, having destroyed the houses on either side to stop the predators getting to him. Each day he goes out and plunges stakes through the hearts of sleeping vampires, and in the evening he returns home before it gets dark, listens to classical music, drinks whiskey sours, and occasionally reads Bram Stoker's *Dracula*. 'The strength of the vampire is that no one will believe in him.' Things do not end well for Robert Neville, bacteria do not save him, even though he does eventually become 'a new superstition entering the unassailable fortress of for ever'.

Richard Matheson was a solid and successful Hollywood writer, working right up to his death in 2013. He's best known in many quarters for The Twilight Zone's *Nightmare at 20,000 Feet* (the one with William Shatner, on a plane, staring out of the window and seeing a gremlin on the wing), and he was responsible for fifteen other episodes as well. His movie credits include Spielberg's *Duel*, and a 1973 TV movie titled *Bram Stoker's Dracula*, starring Jack Palance. He was also the screenwriter for, wouldn't you know it, Roger Corman's *House of Usher*.

Like *The War of the Worlds*, Matheson's *I Am Legend* contains something archetypal: a single, alienated man walking (and sometimes driving) through a diseased world even though it would be so much easier simply to submit. Will it surprise you that Richard Matheson once lived on Cimarron Street in Gardena? I, and others, have made attempts to find the number of the house, and failed. John Scaleri who runs the website Iamlegendarchive.blogspot.com tells me he was at a book signing when a fan asked Matheson exactly that, and it seems the man himself had simply forgotten in the course of his long life. It was a long time ago, and Cimarron Street is a very long street, running for twelve miles or so. There's also a Cimarron Avenue and a Cimarron Way in Gardena, which actually fit better with the geography of the novel, and although I enjoy an aimless drift, a dozen-mile expedition to an unspecified address in Gardena was ultimately too nebulous even for me. I didn't go there, but I tell myself that one day I might.

Again, like *The War of the Worlds, I Am Legend* is a moveable feast. A 1964 movie version, titled *The Last Man on Earth*, starred Vincent Price and was filmed in the outskirts of Rome, in Mussolini's EUR, entirely avoiding the ruins of ancient Rome, although a trashed supermarket and many deserted roads serve well enough. The 2007 Will Smith movie retained the novel's title, and was set resolutely in New York City. But it's the 1971 version, titled *The Omega Man*, starring Charlton Heston, directed by Boris Sagal, script by John and Joyce Corrington, that's acquired cult status, and, like many a cult classic, it has strong elements of camp. The anxieties here seem to be about what we might as well call the sixties. The streets are not filled with vampires – they don't suck blood – but with cloaked, hooded figures, again the victims of germ warfare.

Charlton Heston's Neville doesn't listen to classical music or read *Dracula*, but he does keep up standards by cooking on Sunday evenings, then sitting around in his emerald-green velvet smoking jacket, sipping a highball, and listening to soft jazz, like an end-time Hugh Hefner. The location used for the exterior of Neville's house is actually on the Warner Brothers' lot: you can walk by it if you go on a tour. You can also see it in the background in the title sequence of *Friends* when the cast frolic around in the fountain: the same fountain in which Neville dies.

Once outside his house, however, Neville moves in a real Los Angeles that is still largely recognisable today. He drives more than he walks, but he's on foot enough of the time to make following in his footsteps a possibility, and – full disclosure – various online movie obsessives have done some sterling detective work already, making the job that much easier for *flâneurs* like myself.

And so I began a drift around downtown Los Angeles that would take in various sights and routes from George Pal's *The War of the Worlds*, while also walking in pursuit of Charlton Heston, or Robert Neville: I admit that some conflation took place.

The War of the Worlds section of the walk was actually stranger. You've seen this city destroyed on film and yet here it is, solid again. You walk past the City Hall and there it is still standing, so you know that the one you saw in ruins in the movie was a miniature made of plywood and cardboard. Of course, you knew this anyway, but there's something both disturbing and consoling in seeing the ruin rolled back, in seeing a world that's reverted to its unruined state.

Everyone says how much downtown LA has been revitalised

in recent years but there are still some pockets of amazing desolation and vacancy. I happened to walk along Skid Row, and amid the many homeless people there was an old black man with dreadlocks who was carrying a hammer, and who thought that the tarmac of the road needed a lot of hammering, which he duly delivered.

There's a part of downtown, on the edge, out by the river and the railyards, where I used to go walking a lot, where the roads have names like Industry Street and Traction Avenue, and until recently much of it looked, and was, genuinely abandoned and ruined. It still looks that way in places, but many of the derelict warehouses are now converted into lofts, and the old sheds and other warehouses, made of concrete and corrugated metal, now have signs on them saying 'Film Rental Site' with a number to call. This is a company town, after all. It can make use of ruins as well as Beverly Hills mansions.

Still there are plenty of places where, even on a busy weekday afternoon, you can turn a corner or walk through an alleyway and find you're the only person on the street, which admittedly is by no means the same as being the last man of earth, though some judicious camera angles and editing could no doubt make it appear exactly that way.

Early in *The Omega Man* Robert Neville crashes his car and abandons it, simply walking away to find a replacement, gun in one hand, petrol can in the other. He walks up Santee Street, which becomes a dead end north of 8th Street. The building across that dead end is still there, though it's been spruced up since the movie, painted a creamy beige colour with a bright red fire escape, and it's now part of Santee Village, 'a community of seven loft buildings'. This is the downtown renaissance, no doubt, but the street was absolutely empty when I was there: not even a man with a gun and a petrol can.

A few blocks along 8th Street is the Olympic movie theatre

where Neville obsessively watches *Woodstock*, and stares ambivalently at a performance by Country Joe and the Fish, as many have. A shop selling ornate home furnishings now operates in the building – mirrors, statues, dodgy mass-produced paintings – 'Everything Must Go. 50% to 70% Off' – but the marquee is still there above the shopfront, ready to display any coming attractions. And if Neville had gone just a couple of blocks farther still, along to Hill Street, he could have stood and walked exactly where Gene Barry did in *The War of the Worlds*, and where I also stood and walked. That Fruit of the Loom sign is gone but the building that displayed it looks solid as ever, and very much as it did in 1953.

I found this reassuring. I found this thrilling. There's something immensely satisfying about walking in 'ruins' that aren't in fact ruined. Movies always occupy a space that is partly real, partly invented, and to walk where the fictional Dr Clayton Foster and Robert Neville, and the real Gene Barry and Charlton Heston, did is to walk in both worlds.

My *Omega Man* walk finally took me to the Water and Power Building, at First Street and Hope, a structure that wasn't built till a good decade after Pal's *The War of the Worlds*. It's an elegant, sixties', sixteen-storey glass-and-concrete box, hard to see from many of the nearby streets because it's tucked in behind Gehry's Disney Hall, and in the normal run of events you're not likely to go there unless you have some business concerning water and power. In itself it looks totally unchanged from the movie, though there are some new skyscrapers visible on the horizon behind it. Neville goes there to run laps apparently, though he may be joking about that, but he's also there to do his daily killing of the infected inhabitants lurking inside the building, and when you think of the number of floors and offices in this block alone, you realise what an impossible task he had on his hands, and you understand why he was doomed to fail.

Walking around the Water and Power Building, which is surrounded by a kind of moat containing fountains and metal sculpture, the chances are that you'll be alone, and, on the day I walked my own circuit, the sun was setting, staining the building's glass walls an intense, warm orange. It was easy to think that being a walker in the deserted city, even being the last man on earth, wasn't such a terrible thing; just as long as the vampires or Martians weren't about to appear and get me.

* * *

There was an odd period of my life, much longer than I'd have liked, when I would wake on certain mornings and find that I couldn't walk. There would be a terrible pain in my ankle or the arch of my foot or my toes, and it hurt so much that I couldn't put one foot in front of the other. The first time it happened – a hot, stabbing pain in the back of the heel – I managed to get to a casualty department in a London hospital, and they gave me a couple of crutches, sent me home and told me to make an appointment with my GP, which I did.

By the time I got to see him the pain had gone: if it hadn't, then I wouldn't have been able to get to the doctor's surgery to see him. He reckoned I had tendonitis, which as far as I can tell pretty much means it hurts when you walk, but he sent me to a physiotherapist who massaged me and ran some Faradic current through my ankle and I was just fine until the next time. When it happened again, the pain was higher in the ankle, and I saw a different doctor who told me I was suffering from bursitis. He gave me some drugs. It happened again, in the arch of the foot this time – a new different doctor, who diagnosed *plantar fasciitis.* No doubt it didn't help that the symptoms kept presenting in different places and forms each time. This continued for years.

I got on with my life, accepting these pains as part of the general misery of change and decay that comes with ageing, the first stage of the inevitable slide into ruin, into being unable to walk. A visit to the footcare section of any chemist assured me I was far from alone in my sufferings. I'd see all the sprays and powders, the cushioned inner soles, the toe straighteners, the arch supports, the bunion pads, the corn plasters, and I tried to tell myself it could all be a lot worse, that I was part of a legion, but I also had the sense that these episodes were becoming more frequent.

This coincided with a period in my life when I was courting a woman in New York (reader, I married her), flying back and forth from London at irregular but frequent intervals: 'dividing my time' as the author biographies have it. There seemed to be something about the stress of flying that made things worse. There was one occasion when I arrived back in England and for two weeks could barely hobble to the corner shop. And often the same thing would happen when I first arrived in the United States. For a man who made some claims to be, who had some reputation as, an enthusiastic walker, there was humiliation as well as pain.

Returning to the States on one occasion just before Christmas and getting a new, more intense version of the old familiar symptoms, I could see that I wasn't going to be even remotely mobile through the holidays if I didn't have the support of a cane, and in healthier times I happened to have walked by a shop that had cheap but exotic walking sticks in the window, including some bearing Lucite handles, with a spider set in them. My wife lovingly bought me one of those. It looked pretty sharp and stylish, and it was some help in getting around.

And then after I'd had it about a week I realised that the handle unscrewed, the cane was hollow metal, and there was a sword-like blade hidden inside. That made it seem even sharper and more stylish, and I could certainly see the attractions of walking along with a cane that contained a spider and a concealed weapon. It was an affectation a man might get used to.

But I gave it up as soon as my foot got better. I didn't want to use the stick as part of a pose. I reckoned that one of these days I might really need a cane full-time, and that using one before it was absolutely necessary would somehow turn me into an old man, a walking ruin, before my time. When I was feeling especially depressed about being unable to walk, I told myself that this disability, temporary for now, was an intimation of the future, a glimpse of a time when I would be such a ruin that I wouldn't be able to do any walking whatsoever.

* * *

Well, long story cut short – I got over it. At last I found the right doctor who confirmed what I had begun to suspect, that despite some 'nonstandard presentation' and earlier diagnoses to the contrary, I was suffering from gout. Gout! Gout: a condition inevitably and irredeemably associated with debauchery and decadence. If only. Hippocrates called it 'the unwalkable disease', (accurate as far as it goes) and Galen (the gladiators' surgeon) reckoned it was caused by the accumulation of humours in the afflicted part. He was wrong about that. Gout is simply a form of arthritis caused by high levels of uric acid in the body. The acid is deposited as crystals in the joints and surrounding areas. It isn't strictly curable, but it can be pretty thoroughly controlled by taking a daily dose of allopurinol, which I now do. But allupurinol wasn't available to the general population until the 1960s, so gout had plenty of time to develop a mythology that makes many other, more modern, and far worse, conditions seem decidedly unsung.

A not quite random sample of famous gout sufferers, and therefore of those who were unable to walk at certain times in their lives, includes Benjamin Franklin, Leonardo da Vinci, Oliver Cromwell, Galileo, Thomas Jefferson and Karl Marx. As late as 1926, in his book *A Study of British Genius*, Havelock Ellis was happy to confirm the connection between genius and gout. It 'occurs so often,' he writes, 'in such extreme forms, and in men of such pre-eminent intellectual ability, that it is impossible not to regard it as having a real association with such ability.' Again – if only. It has generally been thought of as a mostly male affliction, though that's changed in recent years.

I can testify that persistent gout, and the persistent inability to walk, is likely to lead to a profoundly uncharitable attitude towards your fellow men. The line, 'Exterminate all the brutes!' was written by that famous gout sufferer Joseph Conrad who, according to the biographies, picked up 'malarial gout' while in the Belgian Congo, some years before he wrote *Heart of Darkness.* Conrad's fiction makes no mention of gout. (I confess I haven't read every word of every Conrad novel, but this information comes from the magisterial volume *Gout: The Patrician Malady* by Roy Porter and G. S. Rousseau, and that's good enough for me.) Conrad saved the topic for his letters. In 1905 he wrote to Sir Sidney Colvin, 'There comes a point when disease like bad weather at sea becomes in sailor parlance, unmanageable; there were four days when I had to lie on my back as helpless as a waterlogged and dismasted hulk.' The notion that his vision of 'The horror! The horror!' might be a personal response to gout pain is certainly reductive, but far from inconceivable.

Bram Stoker was certainly a gout sufferer, as was one of his characters in *Dracula*, Jonathan Harker's employer, Peter Hawkins. I have no evidence that Edgar Allan Poe or H. G. Wells were gout sufferers, though they both mention it in their works, and in a film treatment Wells wrote for *Things To Come*, in the mid 1930s, three old men sing a song celebrating science's triumph over gout (and over rheumatism and tooth decay as well).

* * *

I do so want Edgar Allan Poe to have been a gout sufferer: it would be so fitting, but afflicted though he surely was, this was not one of his afflictions; quite apart from gout, and quite apart from having written 'The Man of the Crowd', he holds a special place in the annals of painful, doomed and ruined pedestrianism, because of the way he died. On 27 September 1849, he set off from Richmond, Virginia heading, via Baltimore, for his home in New York: the trip was to raise funds for his magazine *The Stylus*. He evidently made it to Baltimore, though whether directly we can't be sure (he may have visited Philadelphia on the way), but in any case what happened to him once he got there is certainly a mystery, and at this point in history an apparently unsolvable one, though there have been plenty of speculative and fictional solutions.

We do know, however, that on 3 October he was found in a very bad way, delirious, weary from walking the streets of Baltimore and wearing cheap clothes that were not his own; eventually he had pitched up outside, then inside, Ryan's Tavern, sometimes known as Gunner's Hall. Some reports have him sober, others have him in a state of drunken collapse. He was taken to the Washington College Hospital, and died there on October 7, never having recovered sufficiently to give an account of himself. Death certificates were not required at that time and place, and the local newspaper, the *Baltimore Clipper*, reported that his death was caused by 'congestion of the brain', which may, or may not, have been a euphemism for alcoholic poisoning. A recent theory suggests Poe actually died of rabies.

These days everybody knows that Poe was a debauched wreck, a conflation of the man and his work, but most of this 'knowledge' comes from an obituary printed in the *New York Tribune*, attributed to one 'Ludwig', actually Rufus Wilmot Griswold, once Poe's friend, then his rival in love and letters, and eventually his posthumous enemy, as well as the posthumous literary executor who did his best to ruin Poe's reputation. Among other charges Ludwig laid against Poe, was that Poe often walked the streets, either in 'madness or melancholy', mumbling and cursing to himself; to which any self-respecting *flâneur*, or even a man of the crowd, and certainly I, would respond, 'Well, what the hell's wrong with that?'

* * *

Do I enjoy walking in ruins because I think of myself as a bit of a ruin who is soon to be rather more of one? Do I associate the ruin of the self with the ruins of the world, the way Poe does? Well yes, I suppose I do, though other associations seem just as relevant. The fact is, there are always metaphoric, and sometimes symbolic, elements that go along with walking in ruins. The tropes come thick and fast: we are all walking towards ruin, towards the scrapheap and the graveyard, towards oblivion and extinction, to a time and a place where we'll no longer be capable of walking.

That's all true enough, but I'm not sure we really need to walk in ruins to be reminded of the world's and our own transience. Surely we only have to look at our own family, look at those roof tiles that need replacing, watch an old movie featuring a now dead movie star, look at ourselves in the mirror, in order to achieve very much the same effect. But walking in ruins is more fun than that.

Sometimes, and perhaps fortunately, the metaphor is double-edged, about endurance as well as transience. We look at the remains of things past, and just as Albert Speer, and possibly Adolf Hitler, would have wished, we are actually impressed by those ruins. We don't look at the Coliseum and think, 'What a shame it's not complete.' We look at the Coliseum and say, 'How amazing that so much of it still stands and still looks so good, even in ruins, even after all this time.'

The fact is, walking in ruins inevitably makes you feel better. It makes you feel more alive. Yes, you think to yourself, yes, one day I and everything I know and value will be as ruined as this barn or bunker or bomb-site, but it hasn't happened yet. These ruins I'm looking at are sad, melancholy, and perhaps tragic, they're signs of destruction, the aftermath and signifier of terrible things that have happened; but they haven't happened to *me*, as is proved by the fact that I'm still able to walk in them.

And one thing above all that walking in ruins does is affirm that it's not the whole world that's in ruins. If it were, then it would be impossible and meaningless to single out a discrete feature, building or landscape and call that a ruin. If the world *contains* ruins it cannot itself be wholly ruined. There's consolation in that.

* * *

My wife and I were walking on the shores of the Salton Sea, an inland body of water, below sea level, in Southern California, about twenty miles from the Mexican border. It's a place of spectacular, glorious, unsettling ruin. Parts of it were briefly, in the 1960s, a holiday resort. Some, though in fact never all that many, Angelinos would go there to sail, fish, waterski, run speedboats, and hang out at the North Shore Beach Yacht Club, a mid-century architectural folly designed by Albert Frey; all streamlined moderne playhouse curves and sheets of corrugated metal.

The remains of some of the good times are still in evidence, or were the last time I went there: a two-storey ruined motel, deep in bougainvillaea, an empty swimming pool covered in graffiti, a shuffleboard court, and that yacht club building still stands. Most of these places are accessible most of the time. Fences and Keep Out signs go up and are ignored or knocked down. There have been times when you could easily walk inside the old yacht club, admire the flaking decor, the sagging ceilings, even pick up some pieces of the club's old paperwork. For a long time I held on to a bar bill I'd found there: two whiskey sours and a beer for a very reasonable price. Then one day I wondered exactly why I was keeping it, and threw it away. Now I wish I hadn't, especially since there's a plan to turn the building into a kind of museum, to 'save' it from ruin.

The Salton Sea is not exactly man-made, though it's not exactly 'natural' either. It was created when a dyke broke, and dammed water from the Colorado River flooded into what had been an ancient dry lake bed. These days the water is chiefly run off from nearby agricultural operations, which makes it heavy with minerals, and although a certain amount of rain finds its way into the sea, there's no river or fresh water feeding into it, and no outflow either.

And that's the problem. The water gets saltier all the time. When water levels are high the concentration of salts is low enough to sustain life. Fish and birds thrive there. But as the summer heats up, much of the water evaporates and what's left becomes ever more concentrated. The fish die, then the birds die. At certain times of the year the water's edge is lined with a broad beach of whole dead fish, dried by the sun, like an endless buffet of Bombay ducks, scattered here and there with the skeletons of birds. Inevitably there's often an accompanying stink. It seems a thoroughly ruined place.

I like it a lot, and a certain number of other people do too. Some even live there, outsiders of one sort or another; some in houses, some in trailers, and as with Jaywick, in Essex, it appears that the house-proud and the house-indifferent live in close proximity. And as in Barstow, it can be hard to tell which places are lived in and which not. The best clue may be the cars. Every home, lived in or not, has a litter of vehicles around it, sometimes half a dozen wrecks, but once in a while there'll be a surprisingly new looking car. It's probably worth spending some money on reliable transport out here: you may have all kinds of reasons for wanting to get away in a hurry.

And so my wife and I were walking by the Salton Sea, the dead water's edge on one side of us, on the other a chain-link fence that enclosed a couple of old trailers, which might or might not have been inhabited. Near by there were rusted oil tanks, a trailer that had been stripped to its bare bones, a dump truck without tyres – I was having a great time – and then we encountered a dog.

He was a skinny, jet-black mongrel, and he was limping horribly, holding his left front leg up off the ground as he walked. He didn't have a collar, and if he belonged to somebody they evidently weren't taking much care of him, and maybe they didn't even feed him, since he was chewing desperately on one of the salt-coated dead fish. I'm not especially good with animals but my wife is great. She approached the dog, soothed him, patted him, made an instant friend, and then, after a little while, we walked on, leaving the poor animal to his fish and his fate. What else were we going to do?

At the end of the day, when we were in the car heading home, after we'd been driving for an hour or so, we both had the same thought: we really should have rescued that dog, picked him up, taken him to a vet to be patched up if that were possible, and if not, well, three-legged dogs aren't that uncommon, they seem to be able to walk pretty well, and we could have kept him as our own disabled pet. Of course, we knew this wasn't really a very good idea, just as we knew we weren't *really* going to do it, but even so, even now, quite a few years later, every once in a while we still say to each other, 'You know, we really should have rescued that poor dog.'

And I still keep the fantasy that he could have become my dog, and every day I'd go walking with him, a man and his three-legged hound, becoming known in the neighbourhood, a little eccentric-looking perhaps, but not pathetic, not desperate, rather benign and likeable and brave. I've even thought of the name I'd have given him – Ruins. 'Sit, Ruins.' 'Stay, Ruins.' 'Come on, Ruins, we're going for a walk.' As with many fantasies this may be better to think about than actually to live out, but above all it would have given me the possibility of walking in ruins with Ruins. Or maybe that would have been too easy. A man who walks in ruins doesn't want things to be too easy. I should probably have called him Usher.

Acknowledgements

The majority of my walking, whether in ruins or otherwise, has been done solo, but there have been a few brave souls who've plodded along with me; and I'm grateful to them. These include: Dian Hanson, Steve Kenny, Anthony Miller, Julia Kenny, Travis Elborough, Jeremy Beale, Lou Beale, Martin Bax, Judy Bax, Loretta Ayeroff.

* * *

And I would also like to thank others who have encouraged me, discussed my work, made suggestions, pedestrian, editorial or otherwise. This of course applies to many in the above list too, and also includes Simon Armitage and Lesley Webster, for having the wisdom to invite me to the Off the Shelf Festival in Sheffield, Tom Lutz, editor of the *Los Angeles Review of Books*, Laurie Ochoa and Joe Donnelly, editors of *Slake* magazine, Rob Lathem of University of California, Riverside, for his expertise on vampires and zombies, John Scoleri for his expertise on Richard Matheson, Erik Morse for having read so many books that I haven't, Jason Oddy for his engagingly jaundiced views about photography and ruin, Jim Heimann for his encyclopaedic knowledge of Los Angeles, on foot and otherwise, Neil Hopper for continuing steadfastly to walk the streets of LA, and Merlin Coverley for writing some very kind words about me in his book *The Art of Wandering*.

If I've missed anybody, I'm sorry; I'll sort it out next time.

* * *

A full-blown bibliography seems a rather quaint and redundant thing in the age of internet research. If you want to check the bibliographical details of, say, *The Art of Wandering* you can do it easily enough without any help from me. Where place and date of publication seems especially relevant to something I've discussed in the book, I've included the information in the text itself.

What I'm offering here instead is a short, annotated list of books, movies and websites, not mentioned in the book, that have informed my ideas and writing in various more or less tangential ways. Think of it as Further Reading.

Brian Dillon seems to have become the 'Mr Ruins' of contemporary-art writing. He is the editor of *Ruins* (London and Massachusetts, 2011), which collects together texts by the likes of Georg Simmel, Georges Bataille, Jacques Derrida, Italo Calvino *et al.*, and does a good deal of heavy lifting for the entry-level explorer of literary ruins.

Owen Hatherley's *A Guide to the New Ruins of Britain* (London, 2010) is a lot more fun than it sounds, and I found his stuff about Sheffield to be spot on, though admittedly at this point we're both outsiders.

I realise I've been reading Michael Moorcock's Jerry Cornelius novels for most of my adult life. While J. G. Ballard was accommodating himself to the ruins of Shanghai, Moorcock was experiencing the London Blitz. My memories of the Cornelius books have faded over the years, but ruin seems a given in the Cornelius universe. *A Cure for Cancer* (London, 1971) stays fresher in my mind than most. It features Kensington High Street being napalmed, following which 'Jerry left the burning city behind and headed up the M1', actually going to Milton Keynes, I think. I also like the movie of *The Final Programme* (1973), directed by Robert Fuest, especially the scenes of wrecked cars piled up in Trafalgar Square, though Moorcock apparently doesn't like it at all.

If trying to avoid the obvious in movies, you might like to try Peter Greenaway's *The Falls* (1980), set in a ruined future after a 'Violent Unknown Event'. *Trona* (2004), written and directed by David Fenster, is set in the California town that shares its name with the title, one of the most gorgeous and scarily ruined places I've ever been, though the chemical plant is still very much in business.

Shane Meadows's *Dead Man's Shoes* (2007) makes creepily effective used of the ruins of Riber Castle in Matlock, another place I used to go with the family when I was a kid; and *Big Man Japan* (2007), directed by Hitoshi Matsumoto, offers a broadly satirical take on the entirely obvious symbolism of the Godzilla movies.

The Japanese, I suppose, know more about ruin that most nations. Hisaharu Motoda is a graphic artist who draws and creates lithographs of what he calls 'Neo-Ruins', images of great cities after some terrible cataclysm. Most of his work shows Tokyo, but his images of the Sydney Opera House or the Beijing National Stadium in ruins are pretty spectacular too.

When it comes to photographers, Richard Misrach strikes me as one of the few photographers who struggles with the aestheticisation of ruin, and manages to come down on the right side. For the best part of three decades he's been working on *Desert Cantos*, numerous connected series, generally exploring landscapes ruined by man. His book *Petrochemical America* (New York, 2012) examines environmental damage along a hundred and fifty miles of the Mississippi River, from Baton Rouge to New Orleans, in Louisiana's 'Chemical Corridor', now also known as 'Cancer Alley'.

I'm very fond of a more modest book by photographer Michael Clinton titled G*lobal Remains: Abandoned Architecture and Objects from Seven Continents* (New York, 2011). Clinton has been to places most of us will never go, and his photographs raise a lot of questions about why some kinds of ruin look very similar wherever they are in the world, while others are very site specific.

There are a great many websites belonging to urban explorers and 'infiltrators', which regularly describe their journeys into ruins. Since these expeditions are at best semi-legal, the sites tend to come and go, but www.opacity.us has been around for a good long while and takes a pretty broad view of ruins. A Russian site, extremely hard to navigate for non-Russian readers, www.netwind.ru has some of the best images I've ever seen of ruined cars.

Tim Edensor's website www.sci-eng.mmu.ac.uk/british_industrial_ruins/ is a loving and personal record of British industrial ruins, with a lot of black-and-white photography – Marion Shoard would approve. Edensor is a man of the academy so he writes stuff like: 'Ruins can be explored for effects that talk back to the quest to create an impossibly seamless urban fabric, to the uses to which history and heritage are put, to the extensive over-commodification of places and things, to middle-class aesthetics, and to broader tendencies to fix meanings in the service of power.' But you can always just look at the pictures.

As a sometime Londoner I'm also deeply fascinated by the website bombsight.org which enables you, with great precision, to know exactly where and when bombs fell all over London during World War II. Tyrone Slothrop would have killed for it.

Photocredits

p. 23 High Street in Flames, World War II © Sheffield Newspapers /Sheffield Pictures

p. 25 Milkman Delivering Milk in Bombed Street, 10 October 1940, Fred Morley © Hulton-Deutsch Collection/ CORBIS

p. 87 Huntington Hartford Estate, 1982 © Loretta Ayeroff

All other photographs by Geoff Nicholson.